Stories from our
Indian Elders

For a better future, know the stories of the past

Lenroy Thomas, MA

Researcher and Media Administrator
St. Vincent Indian Heritage Foundation
P.O. Box 2980
VC0100, Kingstown,
St. Vincent and the Grenadines
Website: svgihf.org
Tel: +90 534 891 1077
Email: LenroyThomas17@gmail.ccm

Publisher: Dornald Lenroy Thomas
Acibadem Caddesi,
Yurtseven Sokak, Alsancak Sitesi,
C Blok D6, Üsküdar,
Istanbul, Turkey

BISAC: HIS041000
ISBN 978-625-00-0134-9 (paperback)
ISBN 978-625-00-0201-8 (hardcover)
ISBN 978-625-00-0141-7 (ebook)

Printers include:
Amazon Kindle Direct Publishing

IngramSparks

CHAKRA
10 Swami Avenue, Don Miguel Road
San Juan, Trinidad and Tobago
West Indies
Tel: (868)675-7707 Tel/fax: (868) 674-6008
Email: dmahabir@gmail.com, kumarmahab@hotmail.com

Dedication and Acknowledgements

This book is dedicated to all those Indians who travelled from India to the foreign land of St. Vincent and the Grenadines (SVG), their families in India and Indo-Vincentians in SVG and the diaspora.

I would like to acknowledge the Government of the Republic of India's embassy in Suriname for their efforts towards producing and publishing this book. Special thanks to Mr Junior Bacchus, President of the SVG IHF for liaising with the embassy to seek assistance for this project.

Thanks to SVG IHF and its Executive Committee for producing and conducting the interviews with our elders in St. Vincent. Special thank you to the interviewees for telling us their stories and to Mrs Cheryl Rodriguez and Mr Colvin Harry for making this happen. Thanks also to Cheryl for graciously sharing most of the photographs that are in this book and to Mr Dinks Johnson for allowing us to use his sketch of SVG's National hero, Joseph Chatoyer.

Thank you to all the writers whose works have been referenced in this book and to our local Indian Historian Dr Arnold Thomas, for his various presentations on radio, television and at conferences. A special mention must be made of our foremost genealogist of Indian migration to the Caribbean, Mr Shamshu Deen of Trinidad, and outstanding Vincentian historian, Dr Adrian Fraser for their input. Thank you also to all those who have contributed their stories and opinions expressed in this book.

I am also very pleased and grateful for my twelve-year old daughter's artwork and design of the cover of this book which was wonderfully enhanced by graphic designer Mr Preddie Partap. Thanks to Mr Partap, Dr Kumar Mahabir, Ms Suzanne Beckerley, Mr Denzil Bacchus, Mrs Helen Bacchus, my children and cousins for their assistance in making this book a reality.

FOREWORD

This work by Lenroy Thomas is a compelling read. Although it is dedicated to Indo-Vincentians in SVG and in the diaspora, it is really for all Vincentians since the Indian population is a significant part of the nation and has made valuable contributions to overall national development. In fact, the first Legislature under Adult Suffrage included Evans Morgan who was then the youngest person to be elected to that body and perhaps still is. Lenroy, who examines the Indian population from the time of their arrival in 1861 as 'Indentured Servants' to 2020, builds his picture around stories told by Indian Elders. He uses as a backdrop a brief examination of the India from which they came and the forces which drove them here to work on the estates. He adds to this also a brief sketch of St. Vincent at the time they arrived.

It was important to get the stories of the elders who are still alive for those stories are important aspects of oral history which are essential to understanding the history of the people who were colonised and whose stories have come to us through the eyes of the colonisers. The author, after presenting the stories told by the elders, provides commentary on each, pointing to any differences from the archival records, both to correct any discrepancies and to identify questions that needed to be answered. A few of the persons who were interviewed were able to provide information about India and the arrival of their ancestors through stories that were handed down to them by grandparents and great grandparents. Others were able to trace their family history from the time they worked on the different estates to which they were assigned. The movement from work on the estates to purchasing land and establishing themselves as farmers on their own land, the education of their children, and the movement into other areas of life and work, and to migration overseas are all important aspects of their story.

Thomas, after analysing their stories uses the information provided to add to his archival research and to provide a picture of the lives of the Indians, their struggles, and their movement into mainstream Vincentian life. One of the things that stood out about Indian families was the change from Indian names to western names. The stories of the elders mentioned that it became a tradition to name their children after god-parents who were not necessarily Indians. To enter primary schools, they were also expected to have Christian names, as it was when they became members of the Christian religions and had to baptise their children.

We are also provided with information about the availability of records from their departure from India, the ships by which they came, and the dates on which they left India and arrived in St. Vincent. He identified the Register of Indians and records in the Government Gazettes and records of baptism as useful sources to reconstruct the story of those who arrived on the Island. Suggestions are given, despite the difficulties, about possible ways of reconnecting families with their Indian ancestry. The composition of and work of the Indian Heritage Foundation is provided. Some of their successes would have been seen in the recognition of June 1 as Indian Arrival Day and October 7 as Indian Heritage Day.

Thomas' <u>Stories from our Indian Elders</u> is an important work, essential for Indians who want to understand their past and their arrival in St. Vincent, but a useful document for all Vincentians interested in Vincentian history and nationhood. His work is just the beginning, adding to the work of others like Dr Arnold Thomas. The story has obviously not been fully told but is on-going.

I congratulate Lenroy Thomas on this piece of work and was pleased that he used oral history as a tool for developing the story of his people.

By Dr Adrian Fraser
Retired Head of the University of the West Indies Open Campus

Preface

The stories from our Indians Elders of St. Vincent and the Grenadines (SVG) are finally being told in this book! There has not been any significant publication covering the history of the Indians in SVG except for limited academic research and articles in various media dealing primarily with a short time frame or a particular location. Many have done brief research into this topic and dabbled in genealogy. They and others have the desire to learn more, especially about the origins of their ancestors and their development over the years. This book will satisfy that need and desire for a broader and more varied form presented in a style in which the reader will find fulfilment and enjoyment. It will present stories from the rich resources of our Indian elders whose ancestors travelled to the West Indies and to SVG, in particular.

There is an urgent need to capture the stories of the elders while they are still able to share them and we are pleased that we were able to get these interviews done. Our children, Indians in SVG, and the general public are still largely uninformed about the story of the Indians who travelled to the West Indies and make up an important part of the Vincentian community. The institutions of the governments of India and SVG, including the embassies, foreign offices, tourism, and business departments will benefit tremendously from the information presented in this book. Readers from various backgrounds will obtain a better understanding of the past experiences of the Indians who came to SVG and savour their remarkable stories.

There is a common thread in all of these stories that is eternal. That is, whenever we are faced with difficult situations, we can either give up, or we can decide to fight to overcome these difficulties. The Indians who went to St. Vincent from India demonstrated their decision to fight the difficulties in various situations and on numerous occasions during their sojourn up to the present time. This book shows how they struggled, survived and succeeded in various endeavours. They were strategic and progressive. On occasions they made decisions to avoid difficulty such as the dreadful famines in India and on other occasions they confronted victimisation by vehemently protesting the conditions under which they worked on the estates in St. Vincent. They were not only resilient but ambitious and progressively improved their standards of living, creating better opportunities for their children over the years.

This book is intended to be the beginning of documenting the stories of the Indians of St. Vincent and the Grenadines. I therefore invite you to enjoy these thrilling stories!

About the Author

Mr Thomas is the descendant of Indians who sailed the seas from India during the last half of the nineteen century (1861-1880). He is a co-founder of the St. Vincent and the St. Vincent and the Grenadines Indian Heritage Foundation and has done tremendous research over the years. This includes visits to the public archives in both the UK and SVG and a three-month course and field trip in India in 2007. He has moderated and administered discussions related to the heritage and culture of the SVG Indians for several years. This book therefore synthesizes his knowledge, that of the forums and his elders to bring an enjoyable experience to the readers and hopefully influence their future life choices.

Mr Thomas was born in St. Vincent and the Grenadines. He obtained his primary and secondary education at private, religious schools in the village of Richland Park. On completion of his high school education, his first formal job was teaching at the same primary school he attended. During this time he was also involved with helping his parents on their farms, operating a grocery shop and making hats and caps. While at the shop in the 1970s, his great uncle, Mr Vincent Moore would tell him the stories of his ancestors. As his interest grew, he was able to construct a fairly comprehensive family tree reaching to his ancestors who came on the ships from India.

In 1980, he obtained a BA degree in Business Administration in Trinidad, specialising in accounting and also took courses in journalism. There, he encountered a more undiluted form of the Indian culture than in St. Vincent and participated in various Indian cultural events and ceremonies. In 1984, he returned to SVG and worked as an accountant with both the government and the private sector.

Several years later, getting bored with the monotony of sitting down every day, he applied for a job as Senior Project Officer, heading the Projects Department at the National Development Foundation, appraising business projects. This allowed him to do field trips visiting with entrepreneurs, farmers and fisherfolks. One aspect of business project analysis he got to love was marketing. In 1994, he went to the UK along with his family and completed a MA in Export Marketing Management after which he worked in the fields of marketing management and general management for several years.

While in England, encounters with the Indian community who migrated directly from India to England, sparked his interest in deeper consideration of the difference between those Indians and those with roots in the Caribbean. He noticed that they had vastly different cultural identities which impact their outlook and attitudes. It was then that he started a deeper research into the history of his own roots. In this quest, he later visited the National Archives at Kew Gardens, London, and the Archives in SVG.

Several years later, on August 16, 2005, while visiting his elderly cousin Mr Osley Baptiste at Indian Bay with his sister, a wonderful thing happened. By chance a few more of his cousins came to visit and later in the evening a discussion ensued which ended in firm steps taken to form the SVG Indian Heritage Foundation (SVG IHF). He was later integrally involved in the operation of this organization performing several functions as an Executive Committee member. This includes writing the minutes of the Foundation, organizing events and liaison with the media. As the Foundation grew, links were made with several organizations and the Government of India. In 2007, he was chosen to visit India for a course at the National Institute for Micro, Small and Medium Enterprises (NI-MSME). His time in India included field studies, travelling from NI-MSME, Hyderabad to various places as far South as Karela. He was also afforded the privilege of identifying some cities of the SVG Indian ancestors.

In February, 2008, Mr Thomas moved to Turkey where he married a Turk, and has since been teaching English as a Foreign Language (EFL). However, he has continued to be intimately involved with the SVG IHF and its activities. He started the SVG Indian Heritage group on Facebook on February 14, 2010 along with eight Indians of Vincentian heritage in the diaspora. He now administers the website team and Facebook group of the SVG IHF. He has gathered tremendous information about the history of the Indians of SVG while performing the functions as the main moderator of discussions on these forums.

Mr Thomas therefore has a wealth of knowledge about the roots of the SVG Indians and experiences that are unique. These include his research from the archives in the UK and SVG and his experience of their culture and life both in SVG and India. He is therefore most delighted to bring this wealth of knowledge and experience to you.

I am truly honoured to have been asked by the author of this masterpiece to write this commentary.

I first met Lenroy Thomas, the author, immediately after the meeting to establish the SVG IHF in 2005 and the publication of articles in the media, which attracted my interest in joining the Foundation. I am eternally grateful to Lenroy for encouraging me to become a member. I have enjoyed being on the Executive as Treasurer for fifteen (15) years, with a short break. I have supported Lenroy from day one when he mentioned to me, he was writing this book.

His book gives the historical background of our ancestors in India and the reasons for their coming to SVG and other parts of the Caribbean, their experiences in a strange land, the disappointment and struggles they endured, the loss of their culture, their determination, dedication and hard work to become independent and educated, the progress and achievements of their offspring and the present situation in their families.

The interviews with the eight (8) Elders are interesting, heartbreaking, funny, highly emotional and spiritual. Thank you so much for readily agreeing to share your journey with Colvin and I when I contacted you. The author critically examines the stories and seeks to establish the facts.

The register of arrivals and family trees are a treasure which we should embrace. I encourage us to plant our own family trees, water and fertilize them so they grow beautifully. I congratulate Lenroy for his indepth research and work for the SVG IHF over the years and for writing and publishing this informative first of its kind.

I am confident this will enhance the image of the SVG IHF and I encourage everyone to purchase a copy or copies for yourselves, your kids and grand kids. You will not want to put it down once you have started reading.

Sincerely,
Cheryl G. Rodriguez (Mrs)
Retired Bank Official
Justice of the Peace
MBA University of Leicester UK

CONTENTS

Section 3
  Analysing the stories and records for future use

Introduction

Whereas much has been written about the migration of Indians to Trinidad, Guyana and other Caribbean countries, the rich history of the Indians who migrated to the smaller territories such as St. Vincent and the Grenadines (SVG) has not been adequately documented and discussed. This book therefore seeks to begin to gather what little documented historical information is available along with evidence from the stories of our Indian elders to paint a fuller picture of their past. It is divided into 3 sections.

Section 1 sets the historical and economic scene in the Mid-19th Century. It consists of the first three chapters which look at the historical setting of both India and SVG before the indentured Indians arrived in SVG and their lives in SVG immediately after their arrival. A summary of the economic and cultural life that existed in both countries is also presented.

Section 2 covers stories of our Indian elders in SVG and presents the transcripts of interviews with eight of them in eight chapters. The author provides a commentary at the end of each interview highlighting various aspects of the experience of the Indians who came to SVG.

Section 3 further analyses these stories and other relevant records for future applications. It includes the last five chapters which give a periodic summary of the elders' narratives, presents some of the current available records, demonstrates how to reconnect the families in India with SVG and its diaspora and vice versa. It also briefly reviews the new interest in the SVG Indians' past and the development and achievements of the St. Vincent and the Grenadines Indian Heritage Foundation (SVG IHF). A discussion of the current opportunities that are possible between India and SVG is highlighted. Economic and cultural possibilities in trade and tourism among others are considered.

Setting the Scene in the Mid-19th Century

Chapter 1
India, Prior to the 1860s

There were some interesting events in the history of India, prior to the first migration of Indians to St. Vincent and the Grenadines. India was being ruled by the British, having gradually taken over the country from the Mongols who had invaded from Afghanistan in the 1500s. The British first arrived in India in the early 1600s to establish trading relations and shortly after the East India Company (EIC) started operations in India. By the early 1700s, the Mongul Empire collapsed and the EIC set up an army in India, consisting of British and Indian soldiers (Sepoys), which gained incremental victories and by 1757, at the Battle of Plassey, Britain established full control of India.

During the next hundred years the British trade with India increased and India became one of the most important territories of the British Empire. The EIC sought to fashion and influence a new type of society more in keeping with their interests and traditions. However, resentment of the British grew as its unfavourable policies such as the disruption of indigenous industries, forced acquisition of land, the removal of Indian Princes and the introduction of high taxes created tension among the Indians. For example, the Indian Kingdom of Awadh (Oudh) was annexed by the British in 1856, the ruler was deposed and several landowners lost control of their estates.

The EIC invested vast resources in the armed forces and not enough in the productive sectors of society which combined with the famines resulted in a stagnant economy. At this time the occupation of the Indian soldiers was considered to be of high status and they considered themselves to be elite with many privileges. When the British began changing or removing some of these benefits by requiring these soldiers to serve outside of India or to use rifles, for example, they became highly dissatisfied.

There were also other changes in society that Indians in general didn't like. Christian religions were being introduced in India which were not welcomed by the devout Muslims and Hindus and there was also a fear of forced conversions. The British also tried to reform the status of the traditional religious leaders and intellectuals. This policy saw Brahmins becoming more powerful and caste differences more distinct.

There was therefore disaffection in a cross section of Indian society and some tried to devise plans to overthrow the British. There is a story about how the message of the planned rebellion (1857-8) may have been spread in Northern

India without the knowledge of the British soldiers. First, a lotus flower was given to an Indian soldier. He was asked to look at and think about it, then pass it to another soldier. The lotus flower symbolises strength and rebirth. Apparently, an ancient prophet had predicted that after a hundred years (1757-1857) there would be a rebirth in India.

A similar story involved the making and distribution of chapatis. This was later known as "the chupatty movement" which started with one person making chapatis then sending to others who also had to make and send to others. Although there weren't any messages sent with the chapatis, people saw them as a signal that something dramatic was about to happen.

During the period 1857-8, the famous Indian Mutiny of many British soldiers and residents occurred with brutal atrocities and the vast destruction of property. The conflict is claimed to have started in Meerut, near Delhi and it is estimated that about one hundred and thirty two thousand of the one hundred and forty thousand Sepoy soldiers revolted. Civilians also joined in the rebellion mainly in Northern and Central India. It is also reported that in May 1857, the Sepoys in the Bengal army shot the British officers and marched West to Delhi. This was allegedly sparked when the Indian soldiers learnt that the grease used in their rifles originated from pigs, a prohibited animal for the Indian Muslims and cows, the sacred animal of the Hindus. However, we have gathered from other reports that this was a planned uprising and not just an impulsive reaction.

Hundreds of British soldiers were killed by the Sepoys and this was dramatically portrayed in the media in Europe. The British were riled up and they sought to take revenge to quell this uprising. Huge numbers of soldiers and reinforcements were sent to North India where the uprising started and hundreds of Sepoys were executed. Properties were burned. Delhi was left in ruins. Agricultural stores of seeds in the Punjab areas were destroyed and the normal structure of society was further severely disrupted. Rich and well-to-do middle class Indians were made poor and had to seek alternative ways to survive.

After the rebellion of 1857-58, the British set up a new system of government in India which replaced the EIC. It stopped overtly showing support for the Christian missionaries, stopped getting rid of the Indian princes and more rights were allowed to land owners. However, the dire economic situation continued due to factors such as the scarcity of agricultural seeds while exports continued to the detriment of the populace. There was therefore a desire for Indians to seek a living in different locations for economic reasons.

This situation in India was also exacerbated by famines during the next fifty years after the rebellion, during the last half of the nineteenth century. These include the famine in areas (Orissa, 1866-67) where up to two thirds of inhabitants died for lack of food. Not only were seed stock destroyed, and the rain did not fall but the British administrators failed to import rice to supplement the scarcity. Some of the other major famines during this time include the western Ganges, Rajasthan, and central India (1868-70); Bengal and Eastern India (1873-74); Deccan/Southern and Eastern India (1876-78) all of which devastated the economic life of the Indians. The importation of rice in later famines in some areas helped in reducing the loss of life in several areas of India.

It is against this background of hardship that the first Indians travelled to SVG in the 1860s. They wanted to escape the poverty, starvation, and the famines of India. The British with its vast global Empire, was seeking cheap labour for its estates in foreign lands. They wanted able bodied workers with a knowledge of agriculture and India was seen as a magnificent source.

The migration of Indians to the West Indies as indentured labourers first started after the abolition of Slavery in 1838. The freed Africans had refused to continue working for the low wages offered. The West Indies colonies then tried hiring the Irish and Madeirans and finally looked to India where there was a source of cheap labour. The Indians were thought to be meek, hardy, and less rebellious.

Indians were offered contracts of five years to work abroad with the promise of a return passage. On January 13, 1838 the first ship of indentured workers sailed from India to arrive in Guyana on the Whitby on May 5, 1838. The British Indian government later, on November 16, 1844 ratified the applications for these early shipments of indentured workers to the West Indies' destinations of Guyana, Jamaica and Trinidad. Approval for the first shipment to St. Vincent was obtained in 1860.

Many stories are told about some Indentured workers being tricked into migrating to these foreign territories. Some from North India were told that they were going to work in Calcutta but when they arrived, they were persuaded or tricked into travelling overseas with the offer of a good contract with wages and a return fare. Others were lied to and there are even stories of some children being kidnapped.

CHAPTER 2

SVG, Prior to the 1860s

The land to which the Indians were indentured to work has also had a long and tumultuous history. The Central American region where the island is located is first known to have been occupied by the Paleo Indians of the American mainland who travelled by small boats to the islands of the Caribbean. About three thousand years ago a group of Meso Indians, the Ciboney, journeyed from South America up the chain of islands leaving marks of their presence in St. Vincent. Later, about BC100 the Neo Indian Arawaks arrived in St. Vincent by canoe as they traveled north to the islands from areas such as Venezuela, displacing the Ciboneys.

The Arawaks survived mainly from agriculture, hunting and fishing. They planted crops such as corn and cassava. They are known to have hunted the iguana and agouti for meat. Their society was quite organised with leaders and communal buildings in addition to family huts. They were described by the Europeans as a peaceful people, whereas the Caribs who invaded the island about a thousand years later were described as warlike. The Caribs conquered the island and controlled it for another five hundred years before the Europeans arrived.

Christopher Columbus, with his fleet of three ships, the Pinta, Maria and Nina from Spain sailed to the West Indies in the later years of the fifteenth century. Falsely thinking he had sailed around the world and reached islands off the West coast of India, he named them the West Indies. He is also reported to have landed in St. Vincent on January 22nd, 1498 but this is disputed by some historians who contend that he was in Europe on that day and that he had never actually visited St. Vincent. Columbus is reputed as having "discovered" the New World which includes the West Indies. This area of the globe was supposedly new to Europeans and others in the eastern hemisphere. However, this is disputed by those claim that trade existed many years earlier between some African countries and the Caribbean.

One historian, Dr Ivan Sertima, has demonstrated from evidence found on the islands of the Caribbean and South America that Africans traded with the Caribbean long before the Europeans came. This evidence includes metal arrowheads that appeared to originate from Africa. The proportion of the material in the metal arrowheads found on islands in the Caribbean when the Europeans arrived and those in Africa were identical. Columbus himself also reported that the natives of Hispaniola told him that black-skinned people from the South East traded gold-tipped metal spares with them. Africans were also seen in

South America when Europeans were "discovering" the New World. Statues (olmec) of distinctly African face profiles were also present in South America before Columbus arrived.

I was fortunate to be a part of the discovery in 1997 of an artifact when the old National Abattoir in Kingstown, St. Vincent was being demolished to accommodate the expansion and beautification of Bay Street. I was managing the national fish and meat markets on the same property. While the backhoe operators were digging out the foundation of the old building, a fish vendor who was looking on noticed an unusual item in the rubble. He brought the item to me which I later gave to Dr Earl Kirby to preserve in our National museum. Incidentally, we had a good relationship as my first daughter Nyla used to attend his wife's preschool. Dr Kirby was a Chairman of the St. Vincent Archaeology Society, Director of the National Museum and he wrote books about the black Caribs and the history of St. Vincent.

After extensive discussion with Dr Kirby, he concluded that this artifact must have been of African origin, possibly Malian. On the left is a picture of the artifact, now held at the National Museum, St. Vincent. Dr Kirby pointed out that there were also similar artifacts found in Barrouallie to support his theory. His theory is also reported in the Historical and Archaeological Society (HAS) of St. Vincent and the Grenadines publication, % University of the West Indies (UWI) Number 1 of May 2002. He also relayed the story of the famous African King's son, Abu Bakr II from the Kingdom of Mali, who travelled with about two hundred boats full of men and supplies to discover new lands west of Africa in 1311.

Africans could have landed in St. Vincent before the Europeans and intermarried but it is claimed that the first Africans to have arrived were escaped slaves from Barbados and from a Spanish ship, the Palmira that sank between Barbados and St. Vincent in 1635. It is also claimed that this ship sank in 1673. First, we have to question how the slaves could have swam when they were usually held together on board in heavy chains. Secondly, records of the date of manufacture and company that manufactured that ship prior to 1673 are yet to be found.

Anyway, by whatever means the first Africans arrived in Saint Vincent, they were apparently present before the Europeans brought them as slaves, and the Garifuna people were born. Garifuna are the descendants of the indigenous Kalina (Caribs) and Africans. The name Carib instead of Kalina was given by the French who had occupied St. Vincent for some time. St. Vincent was one of the last islands in the Caribbean to be occupied by the Europeans because of the fierce defence by these local inhabitants.

After the discovery of the New World by the Europeans, several European nations staked their claims in the Caribbean. Conflicts ensued between the French, Dutch and the British, each claiming the island of St. Vincent over a period of several years, but in 1763 St. Vincent became a British colony under the Treaty of Paris. Ten years later, in 1773, the Caribs revolted against the British. The revolt was subdued in 1776. In spite of the Treaty of Paris, the French did not give up their claim to the island and seized it in 1779. However, at the Treaty of Versailles, it was restored to the British.

During the period 1795 to 1797, The Second Carib War transpired between the British and an alliance of the aboriginal Caribs, Garifuna and slaves (Maroons) who had escaped from the plantations. The Paramount Chief of the Caribs, Joseph Chatoyer who had organised a strategic and fierce offensive against the British was killed on March 14th, 1795 and the British again, gained full control of the Island. Over four thousand Garifuna were transported and exiled to the island of Roatan off the coast of Belize, among them Chatoyer's daughter, Gulisi. The Garifuna have since multiplied vastly and spread to other parts of Central and North America. On the left is a portrayal of Joseph Chatoyer, SVG National Hero drawn by Vincentian Artist Mr Dinks Johnson. March 14th was declared National Heroes Day in St. Vincent in honour of the Paramount Carib Chief Chatoyer.

Wars between the French and the British were mainly motivated by the need for agricultural lands in tropical countries to grow sugar cane to supply sugar to their European home countries. There was a good demand for this commodity and the business was lucrative. Hence plantations or estates were set up in overseas territories to grow cane and manufacture sugar. First, labour was sourced from Africa by means of the triangular slave trade. The British traders would sail from Bristol, Liverpool or Glasgow to West Africa with manufactured goods such as cloth, beer, iron and guns which they would exchange for enslaved Africans. They would then journey to the Caribbean where they would sell the slaves to the planters and buy sugar, molasses and other goods to be taken back to Britain and sold. British sailors had been involved in this trade since the sixteenth century and by the abolition of slavery in the mid-1830s, thousands of slaves had been taken to St. Vincent to work on the estates.

The estates in St. Vincent were owned and operated by only a few landowners. Life for the slaves on these estates was gruelling, with long hours of work in the hot sun under the watchful eyes of un-sympathising overseers who did not hesitate to use the whip. The slaves were poorly fed and often suffered from malnutrition and various diseases. When Slavery was abolished, they therefore refused to return to work under similar terms for low wages. Hence the estate owners made applications for alien workers who would accept lower pay. The freed slaves were therefore not able to continue pressing their demands for higher wages and this caused some resentment towards the aliens when they arrived in St. Vincent accepting the menial wages. When the desperate but adventurous Indians arrived, they were meeting a freed but very aggrieved people and the unscrupulous and exploitative planters and overseers.

Below is an excerpt of Vincentian historian, Dr Adrian Fraser's address at the 158th Anniversary of Indian Arrival Day Awards Ceremony and Cultural Event held at the Rawacou Beach Resort on Sunday, June 2nd, 2019. This section of his address is entitled, "What was St. Vincent like when they (the Indians) arrived?" It also gives a preview of the life of the Indians from Indentureship and onwards which will be discussed in more detail in this book.

"What was St. Vincent like when they (the East Indians) arrived?

St. Vincent in the 1860s was in a state of economic decay caused by a depression in the Sugar Industry, the main backbone of the economy. Some estates, among them, Orange Hill, and Waterloo, had stopped production. Many others were in difficulty. Workers on the estates were dissatisfied and had been showing so immediately after emancipation, disgusted with the wages they were being offered and the general conditions that existed. The planters' first response was not to reorganise their estates, but to reduce the cost of production through low wages. This did not go down well with the workers who were becoming increasingly militant. Some began moving away from the estate into villages that they were beginning to establish. They still depended, however, on work on the estates. Those not living in estate houses were in a better position to bargain for wages. This antagonised the planters who did not want to give into their demands, and so lost the control they always had.

Having indentured labourers was a way out of that situation. It is said that Indian immigrants came here to fill gaps created by a shortage of labour. The story was not that simple, rather not true. Remember, too, that preceding your ancestors, were African and Portuguese indentured immigrants who had been coming from the 1840s. The first arrival of Indians was, as we acknowledge today, on June 2, 1861. Interestingly by October, the Lieutenant Governor was complaining that despite the eagerness for immigrants there was an unwillingness to readily accept them when they arrived, each hoping that their neighbours would take. What the planters intended to do was to play off Immigrants against Creole labourers and to provide competition, hoping to maintain an equilibrium in wages. The creole labourers understood this and had become animated. It was also an aspect of the colonial divide and rule approach.

The Indian indentures who arrived in 1861 and 1862 found themselves in an explosive situation in 1862. Creole labourers began strikes over reduced wages and in some cases because of the inability to find work. What followed were riots between September 22 and October 1, 1862 on many estates in the Charlotte and St. Georges parishes where most of the large estates were located. They were sparked initially by attempts to break a workers' strike. Among the estates were Mt. Bentinck, North and South Union, Sans Souci, Adelphi, and Mt. Grennan. Planters' houses were damaged and looted at Argyle, Calder, Akers Hill, Colonaire and Carapan. Disturbances also occurred in the Mesopotamia Valley and in Ashton Union Island. At Mt. Bentinck, Sans Souci and Adelphi Indian and African immigrants were forced out of the fields. In Mesopotamia, Portuguese owned shops were targeted.

Although the target was the planters the immigrants also suffered from their dis-satisfaction. This was not focused on Indians and Portuguese but on Immigrants generally since African immigrants on some of those estates also became victims of the strikers. As late as 1882 Goodluck Clarke, a labourer, indicated to the Royal Commission set up in that year, that they were willing to work "but since the introduction of Indian immigrants they are unfairly dealt with and have no protection even before some of the police magistrates."

There was dissatisfaction by all workers. The indentured immigrants and those who had completed their indenture all suffered tremendously and confronted many challenges. With continued low sugar prices up to the late 1880s estate managers warned non-indentured Indians and those whose indenture was about to expire that their services were no longer needed. The Lt. Governor, however, concerned that an exodus of Indian labourers would upset the labour market urged planters to retain services of the Indians. Housing and health conditions were also deplorable. That was the kind of climate that existed and affected the state of workers, indentured and non-indentured. By the middle 90s an increasing number of immigrants were claiming back passages and over the whole period of indenture almost half of the immigrants had returned to India. Then there were the natural disasters at the turn of the century that added to the disastrous state of affairs. I refer to the 1898 hurricane and the 1902 volcanic eruption where about 2,000 persons, including Indians were killed, mostly in the North Windward area.

The 20ᵗʰ century saw a changing scenario. The indentured scheme had ended. Sugar was to a large extent, replaced by Cotton and Arrowroot and Government sponsored land settlement schemes prompted some more planters to begin selling land, especially on the boundaries of their estates. They were hoping to retain and attract workers to their estates.

The 1911 census stated that the Indian population had become quite naturalised, most of them having been born in the colony, 263 of a total of 376. A process of creolisation had been taking place through the churches and schools. Many Indians had become Christians as can be seen with the names they had to adopt, the non-Christians being among the older ones. With a small population scattered in different villages and on plantations it was a natural development for them to blend in with the general creole population.

In 1882 Lieutenant Governor Gore had noted that free Indians and creole labourers were living in homes in yards in little villages. He said that they seemed to like it "on account of the Breadfruit trees under the shelter of which those little villages have sprung up as well as the sake of each other's company." It is important to note that at least on one ship bringing your indentured forebears here were 14 liberated Africans and certainly some bonds would have been built. This continued when they were put on some of the same estates.

Most of the Indians like the rest of the creole population continued to be involved in agriculture as labourers or peasants. According to the 1911 census, some had become carters with their own donkey carts and some shopkeepers. They had thrown in their lot in the country and despite their small numbers continued to make their contribution especially in small communities where their numbers might have been significant..."

CHAPTER 3

The Indians' Journey to St. Vincent and life after landing

The Journey

The Indians arriving in St. Vincent had just escaped the jaws of hell and the last thing they wanted was to find another place of discomfort. Some would have been wondering if the promises of their contract regarding wages, return passage, and work conditions would be kept. They had sailed the seas of the Kala Pani, (dark waters) passing the Indian Ocean, around Africa and through the Atlantic Ocean to the Island of St. Vincent. Although some ships from India may have travelled a shorter route passing through the Suez Canal which was opened to navigation on November 17th, 1869, the records show that passengers to St. Vincent were at sea for a very long time and would have been exhausted and very weak on arrival.

The ships were usually overcrowded and the passengers were poorly fed. Although men and women were normally separated, there were, however, some good stories of new relationships that were started on board. The term Jahaji bhai (ship brother) has become famous out of those journeys. It is believed that some may have even met future partners on board. There is a theory that one ancestor, passenger Ahkoo, of the Moore, Sutherland, King, Baptiste, Woods and Joseph families of St. Vincent may have met his wife on board the ship Countess of Ripon.

The journey from India to St. Vincent lasted about three months. The eight ships that arrived in St. Vincent carried passenger numbers between 215 and 480. Some historians have described the journey as similar to those of the slave ships, cramped and depressing. A few passengers died on board because of these conditions and also because of diseases. One historian (Tinker, 1993) estimated that about 17% of passengers to the Caribbean died before they arrived and several died after they arrived while being held in the depot before being allocated to the estates.

While several passengers died on board the eight ships, there were also new births. The depot in St. Vincent was located at the site of the current Hospital in Kingstown near to Edinboro Bay where the passengers disembarked. Some older Indians (Mr Osley Baptiste and Mr Samuel Deane) have indicated that

at least one of the ships, the Lightning, first landed at Indian Bay but I have
not seen any records to support this.

Table 1 below shows the ships that brought Indians to St. Vincent showing the
ports from which they departed and the dates they arrived and other details.

Name of Ship from India to St. Vincent	Port of Departure	Date of Departure	Date Arrived	Number of Indians
Travancore	Madras	26/02/1861	01/06/1861	260
Castle Howard	Calcutta	16/01/1862	11/04/1862	307
Countess of Ripon	Calcutta	05/11/1865	20/01/1866	214
Newcastle	Calcutta	??/??/1867	01/06/1867	473
Emperatrice Eugenie	Calcutta	??/??/1869	12/07/1869	349
Dover Castle	Calcutta	??/??/1871	27/06/1871	325
Lincelles	Calcutta	07/10/1874	08/01/1875	333
Lightning	Calcutta	06/02/1880	22/05/1880	213
Totals				2474

Table 1 List of Ships from India to St. Vincent

Appendix I shows samples of the pages of the register in which the passenger
details were recorded and a sample of these lists of the passengers transferred
to spreadsheets is shown in appendix II. These lists show that most of the Indians
were between the ages of 20 and 30 but several of them were families with young
children and infants. There were also many more men than women. Their names
reveal that they were mainly Hindus although there were also Muslims and a
few Christians.

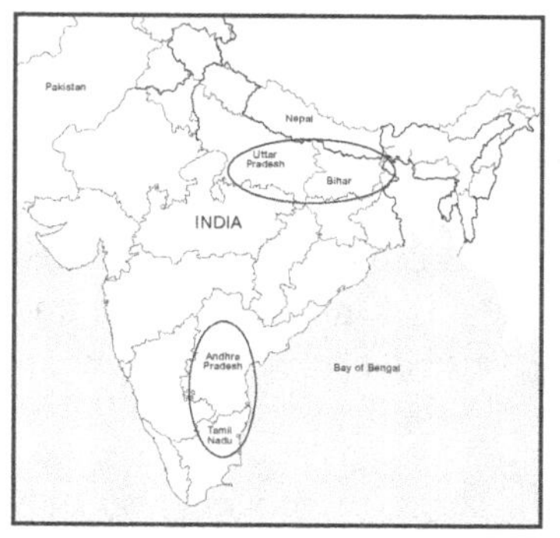

The first ship, the Travancore which departed
from Madras (now renamed Chennai) carried
passengers from the South East regions of India.
These included towns and districts such as
Vellore, Vizagapatam, Salem, Madras, Bangalore,
Chittoor and North Arcot. The next seven ships,
which carried the majority of the Indians to St.
Vincent, departed from Calcutta with passengers
mainly from Uttar Pradesh and Bihar. The main
areas from which they came are circled on this
map. The Indians who went to St. Vincent therefore had some different cultural
traditions unique to their geographical origins in India. There were also Indians
of higher caste from North India who were displaced because of the British

policies, the Sepoy war and famines, who migrated to St. Vincent. The island was therefore a melting pot of these different groups and cultures.

This melting in caste assimilation could be seen, for example, in the relationships of my great grandparents. According to the stories that passed down from our ancestors, and relayed by my older cousin, Mr Peter Moore, my maternal great grandfather, Mr Joseph Moore, son of Ahkoo, was Brahmin. When his son, Mr James Moore wanted to get married to a lady of the Kshatriya caste, there was some hesitation but eventually they got married. At that time the caste system was losing its hold on the island. Also, there were not a lot of Indian women to choose from and the Indians were giving up rigorous adherence to their culture.

Life of the Indians under Indentureship

Before departing India, the Indians would have signed a contract to work for a period of five years. After serving this time they sometimes had the option to renew their contract for three to five years. The conditions of work and living on the estates were stated in these contracts although some of the Indians did not understand the details as they did not know the language of the contracts or were illiterate. Breaches of these terms would result in hefty sanctions and penalties.

Some of the employers/planters were unscrupulous and treated the Indians very badly. Many Indians were victimised and exploited. They had to work hard for long hours and for low wages six days a week. There were restrictions of move-ment outside of the estate except by permission. Dissertation, venturing outside the bounds of the estate would be met with severe punishments. Although there were laws for the protection of the Indians, these were not enforced effectively or consistently as the planters often wielded power over the inspectors and administrators of the government.

Ending of the system

Indians were imported to St. Vincent to work on the sugar cane estates primar-ily to do agricultural work and work related to the transport and processing of sugar for export to Europe. Sugar was a very profitable business for the British planters but with variation in the prices and hence profitability, demand for Indian workers fluctuated. Not only is this reflected in the lag spaces between shipment of new workers from India over the nineteen-year period (1861-1880) but on the estates too. Workers were expected to produce more to compensate for the decline in prices. Increased production in some other countries with economies of scale resulted in lower cost of production with which St. Vincent sometimes could not compete. Another competing factor was the beginning of commercial production of beet sugar in 1879 in the USA.

By the end of the nineteenth century, the sugar business in St. Vincent was not very viable. About forty five percent of the 2,474 Indians who arrived in St. Vincent had returned back to India on several ships by 1882. The first and second contracts of the workers who came on the last ship in 1880 would have expired by about 1890. The indentureship system therefore ended in St. Vincent about twenty-seven years earlier than it officially ended in other British territories in 1917.

The fate of those who stayed

Many of the remaining Indians in St. Vincent accepted a bounty of ten pounds in lieu of their return passage to India. With this and their savings they were able to purchase crown lands. They therefore moved out of the estates and started their own farming business or grew their own food for survival. Some also got wooded lands, from which they cut trees for lumber. One example is the Deane family which moved from the Argyle estate to wooded lands in Akers Hill, a couple miles away. Others got involved in various forms of small-scale manufacturing and trade. Some of the areas favoured by Indians were RoseBank, Rose Hall, Argyle, Calder, Akers, Richland Park, Yambou, Park Hill and Georgetown.

Volcanic eruption 1902

Of the fifty five percent (approximately 1,340) of Indians who remained in St. Vincent after their indentureship ended, many died of diseases and the volcanic eruption of 1902. It is estimated that about five or six hundred Indians died from the eruption. This is a very high proportion of the National total deaths of 1,565 recorded in the Blue Book correspondence (BB1.11 1902 and 1903) of May 23, 1903. This is mainly because many of them were on estates at the foot of the volcano beyond the Rabacca river on the East and beyond Barrouallie on the Leeward side of the island. Some of the estates beyond the river, such as Rabacca, Lot 14, Orange Hill were composed almost entirely of Indian workers.

A cemetery at Torouma, on the Windward side of the Island stands witness to this calamity. Many Indians were buried in shallow trenches having been killed in large numbers by the poisonous gas emitted from the volcano. Although there were some signs of a volcanic eruption, adequate measures were not taken in time to escape the ensuing disaster. Many Indians were caught off guard still working on the estates and died in the fields. One of the interviewees in this book, Mr Noel Soleyn, said that his grandfather, who lived at Lot 14 when the volcano erupted, told him that an avalanche came down and covered parts of Lot 14 and that a lot of people were "scalded to death". His grandfather's mother was one of them who died there at Lot 14.

Others sought refuge in the more structurally sound buildings such as the great houses and buildings of the estate owners. The story is told of some workers who went to the house of a plantation owner North of the Rabacca river. They reinforced all the windows and blocked all the open spaces to prevent the air from coming into the house. However, when a cloud of gas and ash that streamed down from the volcano reached the sea, there was a flashback which hit the house killing almost everyone. Only the planter and his family who were in the cellar were saved.

During the eruption a river of hot ash, lava with poisonous gases flowed down the area now called Rabacca Dry River. This prevented anyone on the Northern side of the Island from escaping and many of those who were trapped suffered fatal consequences. However, a few were fortunate to escape.

A story relayed by a friend of Indian heritage from St. Lucia, outlined how a few of the Indians escaped to St. Lucia. They would have hopped on to any craft that was available and made the journey to St. Lucia thinking or fearing that the rest of St. Vincent was probably in the same condition as North of the Rabacca river. One of these escapees could have been an Indian we believe to be my maternal great grandmother's sister, Mynoah. She would have been 38 years old, and may have escaped with her husband.

Her brother Sreelochum and sister Sewgiah (who we believe are James Thomas and Mary Williams who married Joseph Moore) also escaped but their mother (Hurbosia) was not so fortunate. They also lived North of the Rabacca River but just next to it at the area known as Lot 14. It appeared they were able to run away quickly before the heavy volume of flowing ash and lava got to the village of Lot 14. It is reported that their mother told them to run as she was not able to go fast enough. They escaped but she perished. Most of Lot 14 was covered with material from the eruption.

James Thomas' son, Charles "Charlie" Thomas who was seven years old at the time relayed this story to his son, my uncle Bertram Thomas who told me about it. They later found refuge in the Tourama building. However, many people died in that building covering the children from the wrath of the volcano. Charlie Thomas recalled climbing out from under dead bodies who seem to have tried to protect the children from the volcanic gases.

Diseases and Hurricanes

There was also a disastrous hurricane in 1898 which had devastating effects on agriculture. Diseases such as cholera also decimated the Indian population in St. Vincent towards the end of the nineteenth century. It is estimated that as many as two hundred Indians may have died in the cholera epidemic of 1892 and another hundred of this disease after the hurricane of 1898.

According to the census over the period 1860 to 1917 several Indians may have migrated to other territories such as Trinidad and Guyana. An example is of Mr James Roberts who migrated to Trinidad before 1915. His son Lionel Roberts who is with his wife Rose (Chettiar) in the picture on the right, was his first born son in Trinidad.

It was also interesting to hear the story of a family in Australia who contacted me on the SVG IHF website in 2006, tracing their family roots from India to St. Vincent, then back to India, then Fiji and then Australia. Lutchimin (Elizabeth) who arrived in St. Vincent on the Dover Castle in 1871, is in the first photo below, flanked by her daughters Margaret and Agnes who were born in St. Vincent. The photo was taken soon after they arrived in Australia in 1891. The second picture of her daughter Agnes with her husband Tory James and their daughter Merle was taken around 1920 in Australia. The number of Indians remaining in St. Vincent by 1917 was therefore very small, possibly less than four hundred.

Stories from our Elders

Interviews with our Elders

There has always been a desire among younger generations of Indians to hear about their roots. In recent times we have come to realize that the older members of our families are transitioning without passing down their rich knowledge of our past. Several of us have heard some of these stories but we needed to ask more questions. The SVG IHF therefore thought it highly important to conduct interviews with the oldest remaining members of the Indian community both in St. Vincent and abroad. We developed a standardised set of questions and Mrs Cheryl Rodriguez and Mr Colvin Harry were the lead persons in organising and conducting these interviews.

Mrs Cheryl Rodriguez is the Treasurer of the Foundation, a position she held since it was first set up. Mrs Rodriguez brought a wealth of experience in banking and in organising events in National cultural celebrations. Mr Colvin Harry joined the Foundation more recently as a member of the Executive Committee assisting with publicity and media. He has extensive experience in the production of radio programs.

Interviews were set up with several Indian Elders in St. Vincent and in the diaspora. However, because of the Covid 19 pandemic we were unable to complete all of these. In this section of this book therefore, we will be presenting the eight interviews that were completed and conduct a thematic analysis of the information gathered. In a subsequent publication, more interviews may be presented.

The transcription of the interviews was done in such a way to make them understandable in standard English so that translation to other languages could also be facilitated. However, I tried to maintain the style and cultural aspects of the language of the Interviewees as much as possible, which was generally a mix of Vincentian Creole or Patois and Standard English, which can be coined as Vinglish, Vincentian English. There were some slight limitations in conveying the exact meaning of "Vinglish" into Standard English, without having to restructure some sentences. Therefore, there are some slight modifications in a few sentences and extra necessary words are added in brackets to ensure that the reader understands what is being said.

CHAPTER 4

Interview with Mr Walter Bacchus

Harry: (Can you) tell us your name?

Bacchus: Walter Samuel Bacchus.

Harry: Where are you originally from?

Bacchus: Well, my parents were born in St. Vincent but their parents, which is my grandparents, came directly from India. And my father's side, my father's father, who is my grandfather on my father's side, he was brought here from India, he was kidnapped. As a matter of fact I have this book, which is the Kingsway Histories, right and as a preliminary I will just read a little bit. This is, this carries some of the stories in India.

It said in the time of Frederick the great and Pitt, Britain was busy in Canada and India, a new world of the West and an old world of the East but what do we mean by India, big question, it says while Britain was still an unexplored island lying on the edge of the known world and peopled by half savages hahaha, yo hear? India even then had its fine cities, splendid buildings and temples and untold riches. That was India. This is where my roots are. Sadly, something happened in the history of India that at one time India was taken over by a foreign country, Britain and millions of people lived just what you call hand to mouth existence until they got their independence in 1947. Well, India is on its way back now, on its feet. So, yes. Her most famous religious teacher Budha had lived 500 years before the birth of Jesus Christ.

It went on further to say the peoples of India, you notice what it said, peoples, the peoples of India, however, have never yet become one nation like the British or the French. There have always been many tribes differing widely in colour, creed and language. A great event in Indian history occurred about the time that Norman William was attacking England. India was suddenly invaded by a herd of soldiers who swept through the Afgan Pass on the North West Frontier, India's weakest point. That is now part of western Pakistan. The name of that Pass is the Khyber Pass. The invaders were followers of Mohammed and they soon fastened their rule upon the native people. Again, and again during several centuries, India was attacked by similar invaders. They imposed each time a foreign rule over the people whom they wanted to convert to their own Faith. This was a difficult task. Most of the people were Hindus and the Hindu religion with its system of caste, differs very widely from that of Mohammed. And that still exists.

That's why in 1947, they divided India into three parts, East Pakistan, West Pakistan and India in the middle. East Pakistan had broken away from the West and called themself Bangladesh. West Pakistan is still there and they are more or less not on friendly terms with India. Every now and then they have disputes because one of the areas that India got, Kashmir, is inhabited mostly by Muslims. And that was a very stupid thing for them to do, the British at least. They should have had Kashmir attached to West Pakistan with that vast amount of Muslims because they will never agree to live in peace with the Hindus. My grandfather was a Hindu.

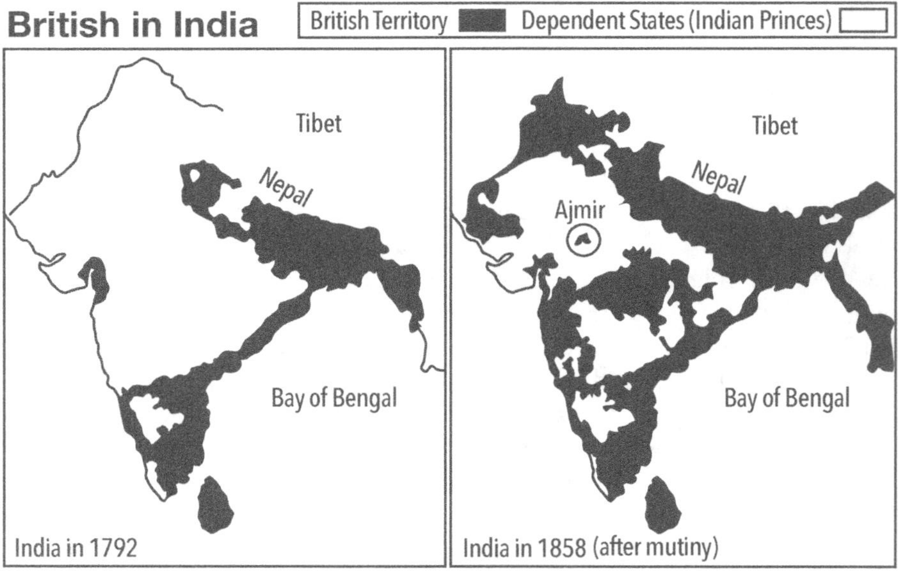

Now, at one time, there was a mutiny in India which was called the Indian Mutiny. If you look here Mr Harry, this is a map of India (in 1792). That's Afghanistan, that's Kashmir, the same place I am talking about. This is where you call West Pakistan. Here is where you call East Pakistan. Right, and India in the middle. If you notice, India in 1792, all these territories were independent territories because look the thing here. British territories, the shaded parts, dependent states. Indian Princes, the white area. England occupied mostly the Eastern side here with a small part (in the West) which is called Baroda or some name. But, look at this (map on the right). India in 1858, if you notice, look at where the shaded area reaches now. It stopped there but it had gone right on. And down here, it has spread in the middle, it has spread all around here. That means to say independent states have been taken over by the British. If you notice here, there is a small state here. I circle it, AJMİR. That's the state where my grandfather came from.

My grandfather was the only son of the family. The others were three daughters and according to Hindu customs, as long as there is a son in the family, the son will continue the dynasty, take over. My grandfather was born in 1840. In 1858, he was 18 years old. He was being trained to take over from his parents as the ruler of the state. One of the things that he had to do was to be very versed in their religion.

One day while he was coming from a theological school, he was kidnapped by Muslims from the instigation of the British. They kidnapped him, took him to a railway station and took him away. He has never (again) seen his home, his parents and he doesn't know what has become of them. He was kept on (a) train. The train went to the nearest seaport. There was no ship leaving at the time. They had that young man from train to train for two weeks going from seaport to seaport until eventually they found a ship in Madras, here, leaving for St. Vincent for Argyle estate, at that time ruled by a Scottish man (by) the name of William Smith.

He was taken onboard the ship and brought to St. Vincent, landed here, taken to Argyle and there is where he remained. (He) got married afterwards. He resigned himself to fate. He got married, got children. One of them, the third son, was my father and he died in 1930 at the age of 90 years, 90 years.

When he came to St. Vincent, he was taken to Argyle and (there) was allotted to him a house. The other Indians who came on the ship were indentured workers. The first week, the beginning of the week, he went out with the others to say well, they will have to give him some work to do. They called him aside and Smith told him, he said, "Look, you are not to do any work. I have instructions that I will give you an allowance every week". Well, he did not know what to do. He accepted that for a little while but then he thought about it. He said that I am living off charity. So, one day he went to Smith and said, they called him masa, he said, "Masa, I don't want to live on your charity, give me work like the rest of my country men and I will feel much better knowing that I work for what I receive".

Well, the only thing that they could have done was to give him the easiest job on the estate. That is a grass knife. You know the curved grass knife. And they put him (in), they said, you (are) not going in the field to use hoe or anything. You take this grass knife and along the borders of the cane fields, there would be grass, cut the grass in bundles and just pack them, put them by the road side and a cart will come and take the stuff to feed the horses. They further told him, you are not to work after twelve, that's the end of your day's work. When the factory whistles, that is when they blow the steam off at twelve o'clock, and the estate goes for an hour lunch, he said, that's the end of your work for the day. You go home and fix your meal. Well, that continued. He was only a young man of 18 years. Well, he continued in that life for sometime until eventually when he became big, he said well, what must I do? I will have to get married and establish myself with a family.

Well, a family came onboard, there were some Gokool, the Gokool family. They are now part of the family (of) the Thomases over at Akers and at Calder. And, he chose a young lady and he got married. And, as a matter of fact, the other Indians didn't call him Ram Balat Singh, they called him Rajah because that's how they look at him. He was a Rajah to be.

When they had their differences, many of them couldn't speak English properly, they would come to him and he would try to settle them as much as they could and so on, until eventually he got permission from Smith to open an adult school in the afternoon. So, when the workers finish working in the afternoon, he has a small bell, he will ring the bell in the village and they will gather at his home and he will teach them quite a bit of English and how to make out little receipts and add and subtract and read and things like that. As a matter of fact, when he couldn't carry on any longer because of age, my father was the one who took over until he left and came up to Glenside, here.

After my father got married to my mother, sea Island cotton was introduced because cane sugar was declining with the invention of beet sugar as the Germans discovered that they could have got sugar from beetroot which is a vegetable. They get sugar from that. So, cane sugar was declining. So, they brought in cotton.

Well, my mother had just got married and had her first child and you might have to call it, a decree was passed on the estate, that all the women will have to go out and pick cotton. Cotton picking usually starts around February. Say, around this month and it must finish in April, the ending of April. (At) the end of April, all the trees have to be chopped down and burnt to prevent any sort of disease from growing up. Especially, there is a bug, a red bug, they call cotton bug, (it was) usually prevalent in those days.

Well my father objected to the fact that his young wife will have to leave her young baby and go and pick cotton and he said my wife is not going to pick any masa cotton. And he didn't say it behind back, he spoke openly. He said, I married my wife to look after my home and my child and myself and she is not going to pick any cotton. To spite him, the house they were living in was (an) estate house, a small board house.

Harry: That's in Argyle?

Bacchus: Yes, Argyle. They sent carpenters. They took off the windows and the doors. They didn't tell them, well, ok clear out and go in the street because my father had no land or nothing at all. They couldn't (do that) but to make it difficult and to see if he would change his mind, the carpenters took off the windows and the door. So, my mother had to go and stay with her parents with the little baby and my father slept in his father's house. My father heard that Punett was selling some small houses at Diamond, and he had a little savings, so he went down there and he bought one.

Well, where would he put it? He had no land. Someone told him, go and ask the Roman church because they had bought half an acre of land and they usually, they used to call it the "Land of Refuge". And my father put his case to the Roman Priest and the Roman priest said, "Bacchus, this is God's land. This is not Smith's land. He cannot put you out. Go and break your house. Choose a spot. Break your house and erect it there and no one can move you, more than God". And so, that's what my father did. He left the estate and he bought this house. He built it there and lived on the church land.

And he had the first child that was born at Argyle, one, two, he had three sons there and two daughters before he heard that this estate owned by a Gunsam, an Indian man, called Gunsam was selling, and with his savings, he came up and bought five acres of land and left the church land and came up here.

Harry: So, your father bought where you are living today?

Bacchus: Yes, that's why I will never leave this. It is a token of loyalty to my parents that I remain. When I came from England in 1971, they were already dead. My father died at the age of 72 in 1952. My mother died eleven years later in 1963. I was in England at the time. I started (spent) 16 years there. I arrived here, back in 1971 and the land was here and I told the rest of my family, I said I am going to occupy this land, build a house and this will remain in the family as long as we possibly can. And here is where I am and am 93, hahaha, yes.

Harry: 93 is quite a ripe age. Tell me about your family though, in terms of their surnames on your mum's side and your dad's side.

Bacchus: Oh, yes. My grandfather on my father's side was Ram. Ram in Hindu means King. Just as you might say, "Her Majesty" in Briton, in English. Ram means King or head. Ram Balat Singh. So, the end of my name should be Singh but according to the Hindu customs, when a boy child is born and he is christened or baptised I should say, he should take the name of his godfather. The thing is, my grandfather had a friend, at stubbs, a black man, by the name of Bacchus. They were very good friends, so when his children (were) born and decided to be baptised, the two before my father, my father was the third son, he asked Bacchus to be the godfather.

Harry: And in those days, you took your godfather's surname?

Bacchus: And they took their godfather's title. The two infront my father and my father. It is not compulsory. As a matter of fact, if you want to take it or continue with it, (you can) but they like the name Bacchus, you know. So, those three sons of my grandfather took the name Bacchus. Two of them settled up in Richland Park and my father settled here (in Glenside, Mesopotamia). There were others who did not take the names. Some remain Bullock because there was one who remained down at Yambou, that was one of my uncles. He retained the name Bullock. There is one at Calder, he also retained the name Bullock. There was another uncle over at Calder. His godfather was Roberts. Well, he took Roberts. But the one which is, do you know Ian Bullock?

Harry: Yes, yes.

Bacchus: Ian's grandfather now, his godfather was Samuel. So, when he became big, he did not like the name Samuel. He said, I prefer to remain as Bullock. So, he remained as Bullock. But the thing is, in the register, the government register, he was already registered there as Samuel and some of his children went abroad. About four, five months ago, I was home here when a group of them came from Trinidad, came here, visited Ian, and wanted to know a little bit about their family. Ian could not tell them very much, so he sent them to my son, who was a teacher living at Diamond, Jonathan Bacchus. Jonathan didn't know very much either, (so) he sent them to me. So, they came here just like you came and we sat down and I told them the whole story and so on, how it was just a custom and they were quite happy to get that information and they went back to Trinidad with that. Many of them got married to some white skin people because some of the children (who) came here were very much white just like Europeans, you know. I believe they were from Venezuela, yeah from Venezuela. So, I am telling you, that is how it is. We continue here.

On my mother's side, my mother was a Durrant, she was a Durrant and my grandmother and my grandfather were from different parts of India. I think they were a little more to the North around the area where the Sikhs are living. My grandfather on my mother's side was a very big, tall, strapping man. They came up here and lived here too. They bought lands from the same man Gunsam and they died many years ago.

Well, we are here, we went to school. My bigger brothers, they got married and so on, we went to school. I started to teach when I was 16 years old, a school boy, in 1943. I had just completed and passed my school leaving certificate. That's the first time they brought that exam in school, 1941. I sat it. One Saturday, we went to town at the Grammar School and sat that exam and I passed. Two years later, the Inspector of Schools, C. W. Prescott came and he asked me. He said, "Bacchus, would you like to try your hand at teaching". I said, "Well, I don't mind sir". He said, "Look, we had no school in Grieggs and we are trying to build a school in Grieggs". He said, "All the children in Grieggs have to go down to Lowmans and it is very difficult for the small ones. So, we are building a Junior Primary School in Grieggs and I would like you to go up there to join the teacher". There was one teacher, a fellow Williams. He was from New Grounds. But they brought him from Myreau. He was down the Cays, from Myreau to take charge of that school. So, with the help of three other girls, one from Biabou and two from Grieggs, I went up there for six months from January 1943 to the end of June and I assisted in establishing that school in Grieggs for the first time.

Well, I was brought back to Marriaqua and that is where I did most of my teaching. And in those days they had what they called the Pupil Teacher Exam system in schools. I passed my exam and my Cambridge and so on. But in those days, I got married in 1947 and I started having a couple of children and I found that I will have to look for greener pastures. So, I left and I got a job as the overseer at Argyle. O. W. Forde, Lawyer Forde as we used to call him, was the owner of the estates then. There was Mt. Pleasant, there was Argyle, there was Escape, Yambou but he had a lot of debts. He owed Casson, Corea, a lot of money. So, he went to the Co-operative Bank in Trinidad, which we called the Penny Bank and they loaned him the money to pay off Corea, under the condition he sell off some of the estates to pay them back. So, he sold part of Mt. Pleasant and a little bit of Stubbs because Stubbs was one of the estates too. He sold Escape and Yambou. And the remaining he had most of it in Arrowroot.

So, I worked down there with him as an overseer for some time. The manager was his step son, Walter Briggs, you must have heard of Walter Briggs. He married a white woman. The white woman was the widow of a lawyer in England. Her husband died and they had just one son. That was Walter Briggs. Well, during the war, the mother sent him for safekeeping to Canada where she had a sister (who) was staying. So, Walter grew up in Canada during the war days. So, after the war and he became a big man, they brought him down here to take charge of the estate. I went down there and I worked with them for some time, then I left.

After I left, I worked with the government. The first Road Transport Officer, Public Works ever had, it was me. I was there and then the fellers were going to Britain and I said well, I am going to throw myself abroad. So, in 1956, I booked my passage and went up to England and spent 16 years there. I came back in 1971. Then, I started to work with British American as an agent. At the time, Teroy Bacchus was the manager. That is Kay Bacchus-Baptiste's father. Family to mine too. Because Teroy's father and I are first cousins. I have to call his father uncle. So, I worked there with British American for some years. But then, Jochim, some Bajan people came and put down an asphalt factory right down at the bottom there. Mixing plants and so on and they wanted a good time-keeper. So, I left British American and I worked here because I was living right here and the job was right here. You know. So, I worked there until they moved and with that I just retired and so on. Yeah.

Harry: What do you remember about growing up? Your time growing up, going to school, the community you grew up with and your close family etc. What do you remember most about those things?

Bacchus: Well, my family, as a matter of fact, the Methodist Church with their missionaries and so on, they were very active, trying to convert most of the slaves and so on. And the thing happen, after slavery was abolished the same thing happened with the Indians, many of them. Because Hinduism is not a Christian religion. I usually refer to it as Pagan. You know. And my parents, they did not hold on to the Hindu customs at all because they had the Roman church very close to Argyle on this side they had the Methodist church at Mt.Coke. So, many of them attended church, the methodist church especially. So my whole family, more or less, were methodists. It's just recently, a few of them have left the Methodists and have joined up with the Adventists. You know, but we are Methodist supporters and on account of that we try to live within the confines of the Christian religion. That is love for your fellow man, love for God, do what is right and so on. But you know, we are living in a very sinful World. Sometimes, we make mistakes but we should always ask for forgiveness. Yes.

Harry: Well, in terms of some of the things you see changing over the years, you've been around for a while so you have seen a lot of things changing, the way people get along, the families and all of that, what are some of the changes?

Bacchus: Well, as a matter of fact, let me tell you something. In the old days, my father was a farmer. After he left Chapel yard, they called that place where he was living on the church land, Chapel Yard, Roman church. They broke that church down and they built one somewhere else, a little further on but the old church was there all the time until on account of the Airport and so on. Well, in those days the main crop in St. Vincent was sugar cane because you had Mt. Bentick going with sugar. Most of the other estates and small farmers were arrowroot. So, my father was a cultivator. First of all he had a bit of cane but it was a bit troublesome with cane so he turned to arrowroot and cotton and other provisions, you know, other crops, root crops, potatoes and other things and so on. Another thing he did, he always had quite a few animals, cows, goats, sheep and so on and pigs. So, we grew up in a way that we knew almost everything about farming.

As school boys, we learn to use the hoe, the cutlass and the other tools, garden tools. We learn to milk the cow in the morning. We know how to go and change, what you call changing the animals, tying them from one stake to the next. In those days you didn't have to bring your animals back around your home because of safety, you left them out in the field. You never found anybody who would go and take your animals behind your back. You can't do that now. It's something different. We live, we eat provisions. Well, as Indians, our main lunch on Sundays would be rice. You know, we always looked forward to our rice on Sundays as Indians. But during the week, we eat ground provisions, soup, anything we eat, yes. We used to grow cassava, we know baked farine, cassava bread. Sometimes you take the meal, you mix it with flour and you make what you call dumplings. And you know all those sorts of things we grew up (with). So, we didn't have any fancy life.

As school boys, we went to school barefoot. In those days, there were no uniforms for school children, (at) Marriaqua school. The only two schools that had uniforms were the Grammar School and the Girls High School. (In) all the primary schools, you wear what you have, as long as it is clean. You go barefoot. Yes. One thing, discipline was very strict in school. Not now, you see children after nine o'clock taking their time going to school. Not so in our days. In the morning we rushed around. We look after our animals. We get our tea. In those days, if we had madongo, we made madongo bakes with cocoa and milk. We called it chocolate. And you have things. You run down the river and you have a wash, you get dressed and you reach school before nine o'clock because you have an inspection. You line up. Girls in one line, boys in one and teachers will come and see whether you comb your hair or not. You know some of those boys, especially the black boys' hair, sometimes they push a pencil through their hair and if the pencil can't go right through, they pull you away. They say, you didn't comb your hair, you know. Well, with us we had straight hair so we didn't have any problem with that. Then you look at your nails. Your nails got to be trimmed. So, if you dig potatoes in the morning, make sure that you scrub them off properly with a bit of kerosene oil before you go to school. You can't go to school with some potato stains in your hand, you'll get licks. So, those are the things we grow up (with).

Harry: What are some of the other family surnames that you are connected to? Are you related to the Deanes, the Thomas's?

Bacchus: Oh, yes, well listen. There are eight sons my father has. So there are seven: besides myself. There is Vernon, Hamilton, Edwin, Cecil, Amos, Alfie and Belford and myself. I am second to the last. There is only one, Belford, who is younger than I am. And, I had four sisters, Maude, Estella, Elizabeth and Leah. When they matured, the Deanes came. That is Cheryl's uncle. We usually call him Tailor Deane but his right name is Vincent Deane because he was a tailor. And he wanted my sister to marry and my parents gave their consent so they got married. I was a little boy. I remember they got married and they went and they lived up Akers.

After that, Cheryl's father whose name was Jonathan but they usually call him Percy, or at least before he died, they used to refer to him as Yambou Deane, as he left over at Akers there where he was living and lived down at Yambou, they used to refer to him as Yambou Deane, he came, he got married to my second sister, Estella. That is Cheryl's mother. Percy Deane bought quite a bit of land from Forde. First of all, he took up 65 acres of that whole area of land where you see Cheryl living down there and so on, come right up. But when they worked out the money, it was a little bit too heavy for him. So, he came and asked my father to take part because we had a piece of land adjacent to the estate. So, my father decided to take 22 acres away from him. So my father bought 22 acres from Forde and they divided the land so Deane had 43 acres. Well, after that, after he died, the land was divided and so on. Some of the others sold out and things like that. Well, Cheryl is one who is still living on the land, you know and some of the others sold out and so on. Yeah.

Well, my other two sisters got married to two brothers too. Two Bullocks and the thing is it, the two Bullocks, Harold and Chester's mother and my mother are two sisters and their father and my father were two brothers. So, we were very close in the family line. But they came and they got married to two sisters and both of them left up here and they lived down at Yambou but they all died now.

Harry: So, were they related to Henrick Bullock?

Bacchus: Yes. Well, Henrick was the same one I was referring to as my uncle who did not want to take the title of Samuel, that was Henrick's grandfather. Because my uncle's first name was Emmanuel. We usually refer to him as Man Samuel for short. One of his sons was Cecil Bullock. Cecil Bullock married a woman from Park Hill. What was their name again? Arm...I wonder if he is related to you? Most likely, you know. But anyway, Cecil married a woman up Park Hill, an Indian woman from Park Hill and they lived round at La Croix and they had Henrick and the others and so on. So, that's how it is.

Harry: Well, anything you want to mention, that you want us to talk about before we finish up to put on record?

Bacchus: Well, I am very pleased. It is because of my old age and I don't move around too much, otherwise I would have taken a more active part in the movement which is called the Indian Heritage but I always give as much support as I possibly can. And I think they should make a lot more contact with India with the main, with the mother country. And I think the people in India will be very much pleased also to know that there are descendants of that country here who are very much appreciative (for) whatever they have done also and that they are quite willing to be close in relationship with that.

Harry: We actually have already made that connection because we have our connection straight to India with the Ambassador who acts on behalf of India. So, we always have exchanges with the Ambassador. We have the connections in place and having people visiting the motherland and seeing a bit of the culture first hand and bringing some of that back home to us. So we can re-familiarise ourselves with our roots.

Bacchus: I am pleased to know that.

Harry: Well thanks for explaining and talking to me about some of the things that are important to our history that we should remember.

Bacchus: Well, I am here. As a matter of fact, I got married very young and I had my children. I went away and came back but my first wife died. I (got) married to a Carr, an Indian family living down the road here. But that first wife died. She died in 1990. In 1994, I got married to a black woman from New Adelphi, close to Diamond. But that marriage did not last at all. That woman, I think I made a mistake because one day when I stepped out you know, I went out, leaving her, we had nothing (no arguments) at all you know, when I came back I met the ring, the wedding ring on a table and she was planning to pull out behind my back. She took her things and went back home. I went up there and spoke to her and so on. She didn't want to come. I said alright, settle yourself down there and from that time, I alone live here. I, alone, live here. Right now, all my children are married.

I don't know if you know Linda who married Murray Bullock. She is my daughter. When I was in England, I became a little naughty so I had two children with an English girl up there, Linda is one of them and a boy. The boy is Paul. He was down here last year and he is married and he is up in England. He is up in the Midlands. Well, Linda came here. I brought both of them down. She won a scholarship. She went to the Girls High School. After she graduated, she started working at the National Commercial Bank. After that, she got married to Murray. Then after that, she went and worked with the Kingstown Credit Union. She was there as the CEO. Then after, she went and became the CEO of this Royalty Bank, this offshore bank but that bank has gone to nothing. Lynda is also a lawyer but she hasn't, she told me, she hasn't applied for membership here yet. But she already passed her Barrister but she is mostly versed with banking.

Harry: Thanks very much for filling me in.

Bacchus: Yes, it has been a pleasure. Nice meeting you and I hope I'll see you again.

Harry: Yes, now that I know where you are located because I didn't know where to find you. Thanks again and I hope that the information we shared here we, will be able to share it with others as well.

Bacchus: Yes, yes.

Commentary on Interview with Mr Walter Bacchus

Mr Walter Bacchus has spoken eloquently about the historical situation that existed in India before the Indians left India. This complements the discussion in Section I of this Book. He also presented the story of his grandfather and his family, giving details of the conditions on the estates and how they transitioned from the estates and got incorporated into the wider Vincentian society. He pointed out that when the Indians left the estates, they invested heavily in the purchase of lands evidenced in his family. They had to adapt to the wider culture but many of the later generations migrated abroad. He also demonstrated that Indians at that time usually married within their race and had large numbers of children, in his father's case 8 boys and 4 girls. However, of great importance is the detailed story he outlined about his grandfather, Mr "Ram Balat Singh".

"Ram Balat" or Rambaluck?

His pronunciation of the name is quite interesting as several older members of the family (eg. Mr Vincent Moore and Mr Osley Baptiste) pronounced the name as Ram Bullock Singh or Rambaluck Singh. It appears from looking at Indian family names that it could have actually been Ram Balak Singh. However, on close examination of the Register of Indians that came to St. Vincent, there is only one name that fits this pronunciation. The British clerks may have written it as it sounded in English, Rambaluck. I shall therefore use the name Rambaluck to refer to him below.

He was a passenger on the ship, Newcastle, which left from Calcutta and landed in St. Vincent on June 1st, 1867. He was 22 years of age and his father's name was Jokhoo. His address is written as Pasoree, Chanowlee, Benares. He was allocated to the Argyle estate and after his indentureship a note is shown in the records indicating that he collected ten pounds bounty on August 7th, 1879 in lieu of his return passage to India. It therefore appeared that he renewed his contract two times.

If the passenger, Rambaluck, is not the correct passenger, the question must be asked, why is his name not in the Register? If he was kidnapped as his grandson Mr Walter Bacchus said, could it be that his name was deliberately left off the list to hide this fact? Was he truly the son of a Rajah who was robbed of his inheritance? There are some parts of the story that are also supported by the accounts of other Indian elders but the evidence in the records do not support some aspects of it.

Mr Walter Bacchus said that his grandfather was born in 1840 and he arrived in St. Vincent at the age of 18 years, which is 1858. However, the first ship with passengers from India, as recorded in the Register of Indians in St. Vincent, to arrive in St. Vincent was the Travancore in June, 1861. Was there a ship that left Madras in 1858 that wasn't recorded in the Register of Indians in St. Vincent? Ajmir, the city of the kidnapping is also quite far away from the port of Madras. Of the eight ships that brought indentured servants from India, only the first one, the Travancore, left from Madras. The other seven left from Calcutta which is actually nearer to Ajmir.

Other parts of the story are quite in line with information provided by older family members such as Mr Osley Baptiste and Mr Vincent Moore. Rambaluck had religious training and performed religious rites at Argyle. He started a school at Argyle to teach his fellow Indians. The remarkable and vivid details of Mr Walter Bullock's description of the life of Rambaluck also seems not to be contrived. The question must also be asked, why was Rambaluck given special privileges by the estate overseers and why was he referred to as Rajah by the other Indians?

So, there appears to be some validity in this story. Sometimes dates and names of places get mixed up when stories are passed down in the family. Another error Mr Bacchus made was about Rambaluck's father-in-law. Rambaluck's father-in-law was not Gokool but Kowlessur. Gokool and Rambaluck married daughters of Kowlessur, Luckpotia and Bunhoie respectively. Notwithstanding the minor mistakes, Mr Bacchus has given us a wealth of information about the life and times of Rambaluck that the younger generation will greatly appreciate. It would be great if further records are found in India to substantiate or verify this story. I will be happy to know also if I have Royal ancestry, as Rambaluck Singh is also my great great grandfather!

Acclimatising to the wider culture

The Indians brought new religion, dress, customs and language to St. Vincent but most of these faded in importance relatively quickly. Unlike other territories such as Guyana and Trinidad, which had a very large number of Indians, the proportion of Indians to the population of St. Vincent was very small. This led to a fast assimilation into the general Creole culture of the Island. The Indians adopted Christian religions and western styles of dress more easily. Likewise, their original languages are virtually now non-existent in everyday life in St. Vincent. Indian dress is only generally worn now when there is a cultural function with concerted efforts taken to remember the culture.

One thing that has remained is the food, although creolised in many ways. After indentureship, the Indians were able to source some of their cultural food ingredients such as curry and rice from Trinidad and Guyana. Rice has now become a staple diet of the people of the Caribbean and Governments and traders import rice in bulk. Rice was not as popular in Africa as in India before the Africans and Indians came to St. Vincent. Also, the method of preparation was completely different.

My father, Mr Alban Charles Thomas who was born in 1922, told me a story about some Vincentians of African descent who when they first got rice, "they didn't know how to cook it" or rather cooked it differently than the Indians. Their ancestors in West Africa would have cooked the rice and mashed it similarly to corn meal, roll it into balls which they would dip into the sauce of stewed meat to eat. As the Indians usually cooked their rice to remain whole grain after cooking, they were alarmed and amused when they saw the rice being boiled, mashed and sliced. Today this custom is generally not continued by descendants of Africans in St. Vincent but rice for all Vincentians is usually whole grain after cooking. Vincentians as a whole have also adopted traditional Indian foods such as curry dhal, curry meat, curry grains (channa and peas), curry vegetables and paratha (roti) as staples. The Indians too have adopted many of the foods, customs and culture from Africa and the original Caribs. These include cooking the many root crops such as yams and cassava.

The language of the Indians and Vincentians generally is also a unique adaptation and adoption of various original languages, different to those of the neighbouring Caribbean Islands. Whereas Barbados was ruled constantly by the British, their accent was heavily influenced by the British but St. Vincent changed hands several times. The accent in St. Vincent was not only influenced by African, Portuguese, Indian and British accents but also heavily by the French. As some towns in St. Vincent still retain their French names, so does the typical Vincentian accent carry some elements of French.

All aliens to St. Vincent, including the remaining Europeans, the Africans, the East Indians and also the original aboriginal Indians adopted this unique language configuration and the western styles of dress and lifestyle. The biggest identifying mark generally to differentiate a Vincentian from other cultures is therefore their common accent. So, when they began travelling to other countries such as Aruba, Trinidad, Cuba and the USA to seek better opportunities, they would have been distinguished by their unique language style.

Outward migration

Ship manifests show Indians travelling from St. Vincent to the US controlled territory of Aruba with the Oil refinery as early as the 1920s. Some of the Indians also traveled to work for short periods at the American base in Trinidad. Later some of those migrated to the USA after which other family members went to meet them. The 1950s and 60s saw a large number of Indians migrating to England, which at the time wanted skilled and unskilled workers for its industries and services. The story is told of the first set of workers from St. Vincent to the South London town of Croydon. They later heard of the need for workers in the furniture factories in High Wycombe. Hence the high population of Indians now in High Wycombe.

Other friends and family also joined them from St. Vincent to work as nurses and bus drivers etc. These immigrants are known as part of the Windrush generation, named after the first ship with workers from the West Indies to England, the Empire Windrush. It sailed from Jamaica on May 24th, 1948 and landed in England on June 25th 1948. Several other trips by ships and planes from the Caribbean followed during the next two decades.

In the late 1960s and 70s a large number of Indians also migrated from St. Vincent to the USA and Canada mainly to the cities of New York and Toronto for economic reasons but also to seek opportunities such as tertiary education for their children. As North America was becoming more attractive, several Indians of Vincentian descent also migrated from the UK to Canada and the USA. More recently, many of them have been retiring from the colder climate of New York and moving to warmer areas in Florida. After the 1980s gradual migration of the Indians still continues to the UK and North America. The relatively small number of Indians now in St. Vincent is comparable to the small number as that at the beginning of the twentieth century. However, there are a lot more people of Indian heritage in St. Vincent who are beautifully joined to other races and classify themselves as mixed.

CHAPTER 5

Interview with Mrs Theresa Jack

Harry: So, we are here with another one of our seniors, as we feature some of the seniors of Indian descent and talk about their times growing up and what they recall about the Indian presence in St. Vincent and the Grenadines. Can you tell me your name please?

Jack: Theresa Jack.

Harry: Your age?

Jack: Am eighty-nine years (old).

Harry: And former occupations?

Jack: Just a housewife and store worker.

Harry: Where did you live and where were you born?

Jack: Right now, I'm living in Villa but I was born in Richland Park. I grew up in Richland Park but about twenty-two years ago I moved down to Villa. So, right now I am living in Villa.

Harry: Do you remember your parents name and their occupations, what they did?

Jack: Yeah, my mother was Alice Bacchus and my father Joseph Bacchus. My father died in an accident when he was just about fifty years old and my mother died when she was seventy-one years old. She was sick with diabetes. My father was a businessman and my mother was also a business woman.

Harry: What about your brothers and sisters and what (do) they do?

Jack: We were fourteen children and seven of us are alive now. The others died. My oldest brother is ninety-seven. He has just retired and my other brothers are retired too. The last one retired, the last child for mummy retired, my sisters retired, everybody retired now.

Harry: What about your children?

Jack: Oh, my children, they are all grown up and their occupation is in: one is a doctor; one is working in a school. She is the accountant in the school. Her name is Vida Giddings and my son is here, Ronnie Jack. My other son is here too, Alex Jack. And my daughter is here too, Judy Lewis. And my other daughter is in Michigan. She works in the Hong Kong area but right now she doesn't want to go back there yet. And that's all. Seven children.

Harry: Do you know of your uncles and aunts, are you aware of their backgrounds, what they did as well?

Jack: My uncles, they all were like farmers, tailor and my aunties, they were just housewives. I could remember my uncle Norman Bacchus, my uncle Nathaniel Bacchus, my uncle Owen Bacchus, my auntie Mary McDowall, Elmina Williams and Catharine Morgan. Those are who I could remember.

Harry: Ok, that's fine. What about your grandparents? (Do) you remember their names and what they used to do?

Jack: Yes. My grandmother was Mary Moore. She lived one hundred and three years. And she used to live with my parents when she got older. She was blind, she couldn't see, so I used to take care of her when I was at home. When I got married, she said, "Theresa, you going, who's going to bathe me now?" I said, my other sister would bathe you. But she died after I got married. I don't remember what year she died but she died after I got married and I was married in 1953.

Harry: 1953, that's a very long time ago. Where did your grandparents live though, did they live in Richland Park?

Jack: In Richland Park. Since I knew them, they lived in Richland Park.

Harry: What about the other relatives, your cousins and other people you are related to? Not necessarily your aunts and uncles but other relatives you were close to?

Jack: Well, most of my cousins were living in Richland Park but they all migrated. Some in Canada, some in America, some in England, they all, most of them migrated.

Harry: Ok. (Do) you remember any of them in particular? Maybe they were skilled in tailoring or seamstresses or otherwise. In terms of extended relatives, cousins etc.

Jack: Some of them were teachers, some of them were politicians. Morgan was a Politician and McDowall was a politician too but they all passed away. Morgan is still alive but McDowall has passed away.

Harry: And while you were growing up, did you get any or hear any stories from your parents or grandparents about the Indian forefathers? Those who came from India and the traditions they brought?

Jack: No, I don't know much about that. I can't remember much about that.

Harry: Ok, so you didn't really hear much about that growing up?

Jack: No, no.

Harry: Ok. As a child growing up and in your former years, tell me a bit about what life was like for you, I mean primary school days and then after that to now.

Jack: Well, (for) primary school, I used to go to a lady named sister Williams. I used to go to her school. And when I have lunchtime, I used to go over to my grandmother but she was not living too far from sister Williams and afterwards, I started to go to Mesopotamia school. But it was hard for me to walk down there every day and my father decided that he was going to start a primary school, help start a primary school in the Seventh Day Adventist church. So, I was out of school for a couple years but when I was about thirteen years (old), the (new) school started and I went back to school. But suddenly my father died and I didn't get to finish school. I didn't get much education.

Harry: After you left school, you said you didn't get to finish, what happened next for you?

Jack: I was home with my mum (as) my father died helping to take care of my other siblings because I was the oldest one at home. The older ones, they were married already and I was the oldest one at home so I used to take care of the others who were left behind and help my mum with them. Then I didn't get to go to school much anymore.

Harry: What about your early years with your husband getting involved in business, were you being that support with him as well? How was that in terms of from the ground up?

Jack: When we got married, we didn't have anything, we were very poor but my mum gave us a (sewing) machine and my husband used to make caps and go and sell them and this is where he started his business, buying and selling, making clothes and selling all the years. That is where we started business and I grew up in the business and helped in the business until we are here today.

Harry: And today you have Jax Enterprises which your husband and yourself built to what it is today.

Jack: Jax Enterprises is now run by my children because I am retired.

Harry: How would you say things are now, compared to when you were growing up, 40, 50, 60 years ago in terms of the Vincentian way of life and the way how people relate to each other?

Jack: It's much different now than when I was growing up, because when I was growing up, we couldn't eat like what we could eat today. We used to eat breadfruit, morning, noon and night but now we can eat anything as we want to. So, it's much different right now.

Harry: Any special treasured memories, things that you remember most when you were growing up, that you'd want to tell us about, special moments in your life?

Jack: The only thing I could remember about my grandmother when she used to live with us, we got radios in St. Vincent. And then, the radio was playing all day. So, she said in the evening, "Theresa, did you all give those guys some drinks? They sing all day. I want to know if they got anything to drink." I said, "yes granny, we gave them something to drink". Because she couldn't see, so she didn't understand.

Harry: So, you remember a lot about your grandmother?

Jack: Yes, because she stayed with us when I was home when she got blind. My mother took her to live with us.

Harry: You mentioned that treasured memory there, and there must have been times as well when things were difficult for you growing up and in the later stages of life. Any of the hardships that you went through, things, some challenges that you faced that you wish to talk about.

Jack: Not really. I grew up with my mum, tried to help her and everything was going fine. I got married to a very kind and gentle man and we worked together making life easy. I was happy all these years.

Harry: If you had to change anything in your life growing up, what would that be?

Jack: Well, I grew up a Christian all these years and now, I can't do anything else other than be a Christian until I die.

Harry: What about any decisions that you made, anything that you did that you probably thought that you didn't do it the right way that you'd wish to change in life? Anything like that stuff?

Jack: Well, there may be lots of stuff that I could have done and I didn't do it right but I just can't remember everything now.

Harry: Ok. What about the changes you've seen in St. Vincent and the Grenadines, if you can change anything in SVG what would that be and why?

Jack: I would like the young people to be Christians. That is the thing I like most, I would like because they are not behaving well sometimes.

Harry: So, you'd like to see more of the young people get involved.

Jack: Involved in Christianity.

Harry: Ok, and become Christians?

Jack: Yes, and become Christians because if we are not Christians, we can't see Christ when He comes.

Harry: Do you know anything about the Indian Heritage Foundation? Have you heard of it?

Jack: I heard they talk about it but I don't know much about it because my husband is not a real Indian. He mixed. He is half Indian, and then he doesn't want to take much active part in that and he is old now so he can't do much.

Harry: Ok. Did you enjoy sharing your story with us and chatting with us?

Jack: Yes, I did.

Harry: Anything you want to add before we close off.

Jack: Well, I would like that the Indian people get back to the old-time days when they used to interact with one another more closely and talk to one another more closely but everybody is kind of selfish now.

Harry: Ok, so that is what you'd want to see. And that is what the organisation is there to do, to bring everybody back together. At least we could make the family connections and reunite everybody. It doesn't matter if you are half Indian, quarter Indian or whatever. Once you have some background and some parents or relatives that have been of Indian descent, we can make that connection familywise. So, let me thank you very much and I appreciate the time you spent chatting with me and sharing very important information.

Jack: Thank you

Introduction to themes from this Interview

There are several areas of interest that were highlighted in this interview, some of which were discussed in Chapter 3. These include the Indians' involvement in trade and manufacturing and outward migration to Europe and North America. However, in the discussion below we shall touch on three important areas that Mrs Theresa Jack mentioned. These are 1, the upward mobility and changing occupations of the Indians, 2, the development in educational opportunities through The Richland Park Seventh Day Adventist Primary and

Secondary Schools and 3, a brief review of how the Indians became Christians using an example of the Richland Park Indian community and the Seventh Day Adventist Church.

Upward mobility and changing occupations

After indentureship the occupations of the Indians were mostly farming. However, as different aspects of society developed in St. Vincent during the 1920s through to the 1960s more Indians got involved in trade and light manufacturing. Their occupations include cap making, coconut oil and soap production, retailing and export. As primary education became more accessible most of the Indians, like the rest of the population, obtained a primary school education but very few were able to access high school education as there were only two high schools on the Island at the time, The Boys Grammar School and the Girls High School, both in Kingstown far away from most of the Indian communities. Notwithstanding, a few Indians were able to enter the teaching profession and three even tried their hands at politics. These are Mr Evans Morgan, Mr Chieftain McDowall and Mr Donelly Bacchus.

Many of the Indians were ambitious and strove for a better standard of living which they thought could be gained by educating their children. As early as the Indentureship period, the Indians had tried to start a school to teach their religion and culture among other things but this didn't last. Our family has passed down a story that my maternal great, great grandfather, Mr Rambaluck Singh was a pundit or Hindu priest at that time. However, most of the family moved to other nearby villages including Richland Park where his grandson, Mr Joseph Bacchus, my grandfather, was very instrumental in starting a new school, The Richland Park Seventh Day Adventist Primary School, that is still operating successfully today.

The Richland Park Seventh Day Adventist Primary and Secondary Schools

By the early 1930s the Indians in Richland Park had encountered various Christian religions and there was a strong following of the Seventh Day Adventists in the village of Richland Park. As mentioned in Mrs Theresa's interview, the nearest primary school was in Mesopotamia which is about two miles walk away, on a stone road. Efforts were therefore made to establish a school in Richland Park and this found its fulfilment through the Seventh Day Adventist Church which was spearheaded by several members including those of the Indian community.

The first school was started in 1936 with ten students in a member's home, Ms Alice Williams. After a short break it continued in Mr Joseph Bacchus' home then on to Mr Lynch's Hall at Junction. In 1945 it moved into the newly built Seventh Day Adventist Church building, now owned by the Anglican Church. The land for this church building was donated by Mr Joseph Bacchus but later when the membership outgrew the building, he again donated a larger plot of land where the current church was built. In 1962 the school moved to the ground floor of this concrete building which also included an extension made of bamboo.

As the school expanded into a high school the ground floor of the church was used exclusively for a high school, the Mountain View Academy (MVA) from the late 1960s and the primary school was housed in Mr Eli Bacchus' house. The high school was previously at Perseverance, an area about two and a half miles from the primary school. In the 1970s the primary school moved into the first floor of the Church which was expanded with a new wing. As the student population of both schools increased, a new building with modern facilities was built next to the village playing field, Oval to house the MVA and the primary school moved back to the ground floor of the church.

These educational institutions gave the Indians of the Richland Park community and surrounding village the chance to earn a high school education. Parallel to the building of these schools in Richland Park, similar schools were established in other parts of St. Vincent both by the Government and religious denominations. Many Indians were therefore able to enter the teaching profession through the Teachers Training Centre in Arnos Vale. Others entered universities abroad and became qualified in various professions such as doctors, dentists, accountants, pharmacists, economists and pastors.

How did they become Christians?

The Indians who originally arrived from India continued to practice their religion and culture on the estates where they lived. I have heard stories of such activities at a cave in the Buccament area and a place at Lot 14 Orange Hill where Hindu rituals used to be held. However, on a typical estate there were several groups with diverse backgrounds of castes, clans and religious practices (e.g. Hindus and Muslims). With the exception of the Argyle estate, there seems not to have been any concerted effort to organise any formal traditional religious Indian institutions. With less than a total of about 400 Indians on the Island at the beginning of the twentieth century and with no further immigrants coming from India to revive cultural interests, it may have been easier, removed from institutions of their existing religions, to yield to the existing religious and social pressures exerted from the established western religions and cultural influences within St. Vincent at the time.

Not only did the Indians accept western names but they gave their children traditional western or European names. It is said that children were required to have English names to be eligible to enroll in primary schools. New borns were therefore christened or baptised and given western names. These baptismal certificates were in fact like naturalisation records for citizenship. Hence, in this way most of the Indians became part of the Christian religions. However, stronger affiliation with various religious denominations was a result of the missionaries who came to the island.

During the period after indentureship to the 1930s most of the Indians had assimilated in one form or the other into the traditional western religions such as the Catholic, Anglican and Methodist churches. At this time, Evangilicals, Pentecostals and other Protestant religions were having an impact with missionaries too. One strategy used to convert the Indians was to send Indian missionaries from Trinidad. An account narrated by Mr James Woods in an interview with Dr Kumar Mahabir demonstrated this fact. Two young Indian men, colporteurs (booksellers) Manoram and Ramrattan came to St. Vincent from Trinidad. After reading two of their books, *The Great Controversy between Christ and Satan* and *The Revelation and Christain Sabbath* and building a relationship with them, Mr Woods was baptized into the Seventh Day Adventist Church in 1931 at the age of 41 years. Mr Woods stated that his father, Mr Seetaram Woods had died and after the old generation died, the next generation took up "the English way".

Many of the Indian Christains who were the descendants of Hindus were not at this time practicing any aspect of the religion and one older family member, Mr Vertyl Bacchus even described the Indians as having no religion. As an example of the conversion of the Indians from Hinduism to Christianity from about the 1930s let us look at the early history of the Seventh-day Adventist Church in Richland Park as described by my father, Mr Alban Thomas. This church was very instrumental in the development of a very strong affiliation of the Indians with a Christain religion.

The first Seventh Day Adventist (SDA) Missionary (after the colporteurs) to come to Richland Park was Pastor Payne who came to the Marriaqua valley in 1932. He rented Mr Samuel Jackson's house and used it as the first SDA church in Richland Park. My father, Mr Alban Thomas spoke of this time when he was a little boy going to church with his father, Mr Charles "Charlie" Thomas and sleeping under the church organ. The church operated at this site for about six months. The first converted members were Mr Charles "Charlie" Thomas, Mr

Byron Simon and Mr James Woods. These three men were the pioneers of the church in Richland Park and the Marriaqua valley.

Mr Charles Thomas was elected and became the earliest First (Head) Elder of the SDA Church in Richland Park. He was a very motivated and dynamic person and had a driving philosophy to spread the new light he had found but being an Indian of Hindu origin, he was ridiculed by the local Indian residents. Once, they mobbed him knocking "bun pans" and other noisy implements. However, he was a very strong-willed person who persevered and actively spread the Advent message in Richland Park and surrounding communities.

When the next pastor, Mr Wiseman came to St. Vincent the church moved to Mr James Woods' house. In 1935 at the age of 12 years my father, Mr Alban Charles Thomas along with John and Rebecca Bopkin were baptised. The church was still viewed as being very atypical and peculiar at the time. However, it was not until Mr Joseph Bacchus joined the church that it really gained a foothold and the momentum for expansion began in Richland Park.

Many stories are told of the long and frequent lively debates Mr Charles "Charlie" Thomas had with Mr Joseph Bacchus in an effort to convince him to accept the teachings of the church. Finally, one day Mr Joseph Bacchus conceded and marked the occasion by smashing a bottle of strong rum, apparently vowing not to drink alcohol again. Mr Joseph Bacchus and his son Vertyl were later baptised.

Mr Joseph Bacchus was very influential in the Marriaqua community probably because he was relatively wealthy, possibly the most affluent in Richland Park at the time. He also owned the only bus which operated from Kingstown, the capital of St. Vincent to Richland Park. He had a vital part to play in bringing both his brother Mr Norman Bacchus and his brother-in-law Mr James Morgan into the church. They were also well-known persons in the community. Around this time Mrs Mary Mc Dowall of Richland Park and Mr Waitley Williams of Simon/New Prospect were also baptised. In 1938 there was a landslide victory for the church when, on one day, thirty (30) persons were baptised including my mother Eileen Thomas.

By the time the next pastor, Mr Coalhuss came to St. Vincent, the church had made an impact on the community. Mr Coalhuss was instrumental in seeking help from the government of SVG to obtain timber to build a church at Belplen, at the side of the road into Richland Park. This church project solidified the zeal of the members of the church. Many stories are told of the great efforts the early members made to carry boulders from the river and cut lumber to build this church. Pastor Coalhuss only stayed about two or three months in St. Vincent but the church was later completed, built around 1940-41.

The first musician at this new church was Mr Waitley Williams. The first couple to get married there was Mr Alban and Mrs Eileen Thomas in 1943. The next pastor, Mr Braithwaite who succeeded Mr Coalhuss was the first pastor at the new church at Belplen. He resided at Mr Joseph Bacchus' house while in St. Vincent. Other pastors to follow him were Pastor Warner and later Pastor Carrington.

Sadly, for the SDA church, the stalwart, Mr Charles "Charlie" Thomas who "raised up" the church in Richland Park later said he found "new light" which he followed. He later went on to help establish the Seventh Day Church of God religion in Richland Park, forging ties with Mr Sween and Mr James Woods and others. Mr Woods' descendants now play a leading role in that church.

There were other groups of the SDA church that were established early in St. Vincent. These include a "company" in Troumaca (1902) and another in Old Montrose on the road to Green Hill. However, the most vibrant expansion of the church in St. Vincent was in the central part of the Island. Significantly, the majority of Indians in Richland Park joined the church and they propelled the growth of the church on the Island. They helped in the establishment of the churches in Calder, Mesopotamia, Biabou, Evesham, Park Hill and Georgetown during the period 1940 to 1970 and later during the period 1970 to 1985, in Greggs and Lowmans. By the beginning of the twenty-first century there were about 10,000 Seventh Day Adventist in St. Vincent, with Richland Park church accounting for a substantial proportion of that number.

CHAPTER 6
Interview with Mr Samuel Deane

Harry: (Can you) tell us your full name?

Deane: Samuel Augustine Deane.

Harry: And what (did) you used to do in terms of occupation.

Deane: Well, I used to work and cultivate land, a farmer and then I used to traffic going from the Grenadines Islands to Trinidad with the stuff.

Harry: Ok, and where do you live?

Deane: Well, at that time, I had this land at Akers here, but I was living over Mesopotamia, Mt. Pleasant way because it's over there that my wife came from so I was living in the area where she came from, you know, because I got some land and things from them.

Harry: And where are you living now?

Deane: This is Akers, here.

Harry: (Can) you recall where you were born.

Deane: Yes, I (was) born at Akers but at another spot around the other side but the same Akers.

Harry: What about your parents, (do) you remember anything about them?

Deane: My father (was) Vincent Deane and my mother, Martina Deane.

Harry: Were they farmers as well?

Deane: He was a farmer and he was a tailor.

Harry: What about your mum?

Deane: Well only domestic in the home to see about the children and so.

Harry: (Do) you have any brothers and sisters?

Deane: Yes.

Harry: Do you remember their names?

Deane: Yes, I have. I lost some, you know? Rita (is) my sister in England but she got old, she (is) named Rosita and there is a young one named Ancil. Felix and one of my brothers died in England.

Harry: So, some of them died but you still have a few of them around? What about your children, do you have any children?

Deane: Yes.

Harry: What are their names?

Deane; Yes, I have six boys, you hear, and two girls. Out of the six boys, let me see, two are dead and I have a son Mike and then I got Alwyn, that is "Small Lee". He lives down there. And then I have Bob at Yambou.

Harry: So, what about your uncles and your aunts?

Deane: Yes, let me see. Most of them died out too. I know I have one uncle down at Mespo now, that is Walter Bacchus and plenty of them died in England, and so.

Harry: What about those on your father's side?

Deane: None on my father's side are alive, Baston's father, he died a long time (ago).

Cheryl: And my father Johnathan.

Deane: Yes, yes because there is no more.

Harry: What about your grandparents? Your grandfather and your grandmother on both sides, do you remember anything about them?

Deane: Yes, my grandfather. He had his Indian name, you know. His Indian name was Kalloo Ramphul, you know, but he changed over to William Deane. And his wife was named Mary Deane. Well, it's Mary Deane (who) I got this place from, my grandmother.

Harry: Were they farmers as well?

Deane: Yes, they were farmers and they raised their children and all of them went abroad to America, and so, you know.

Harry: And, in terms of where your grandparents lived, did they live in Akers as well or other parts?

Deane: Yes, they lived in Akers, right here. They first lived at Argyle, you know, and after they went Peruvain Vale and then they came to Akers, here.

Harry: Do you know any of your other relatives, other than your grandparents, maybe like your cousin or other family member when you were growing up?

Deane: Yes, but most of them in England and (everywhere) now. They are not in St. Vincent now. I had a close friend and a cousin. His name was Alvin Bacchus and he is supposed to be in America. And he had a brother named Rupert. Rupert got old and he is in America too.

Harry: Did your parents or your grandparents ever tell you any stories about India and what India was like and about the culture and stuff like that?

Deane: Yes, my grandfather told me that when he left India, he was 12 years old with his parents and he was fully educated for (his age of) 12 years. He said they took three months from India to reach the West Indies. But he said they stopped in Africa to buy foodstuff, you know. He said he never saw bigger pumpkins and bigger yams (than) in Africa. And when they left there, they travelled until they reached St. Vincent. But it's somewhere down Youngs Island, where the boat came in and they fixed the boat there.

Harry: Ok, ok, so they told you that they landed at Young Island?

Deane: Yes, yes

Harry: Around the area, Indian Bay, Young Island area?

Deane: Yes

Harry: Ok

Deane: But my grandmother didn't come on that trip, you know. Only my grandfather. My grandmother came on a different ship because she came from Madras. She is a short, clear Indian.

Harry: Did they ever share with you any of the Indian names and some of the Indian names their people used, home in India?

Deane: I couldn't really talk the language so much you know.

Harry: So, you don't remember some of the Indian names they used to use?

Deane: No.

Harry: Your grandparents though, did they live in Akers as well, were they all from Akers too?

Deane: As I tell you, when they came here, they reached Argyle first, and after the destruction with the hurricane, they left and moved to Peruvain Vale and from Peruvain Vale, they ended up in Akers and they bought this place in Akers and lived up here. But it's plenty of land they had, you know, from Akerst down to Mespo. The land is big.

Harry: What do you remember about growing up in your younger days, in the days of your primary school etc and when you were a boy and when you became a man, what are some of the things you remember from those times?

Deane: I went to primary school, maybe when I was about four years and I went to the government school at Mespo when I was six and I finished school when I was twelve with full education from there. And from there I started on my own (to) do little work until I started to cultivate lands and traffic going to the Grenadines first when the market was small then I started to go to Trinidad. And after that, when I reached an (older) age I came back and relaxed myself in the garden because bananas and so (on) were in full existence on the Island. Bananas were the main crop.

Harry: Ok. How would you say things have changed now as compared to then, in terms of how you are now? Is it easier now, or were those times easier for you?

Deane: Well, right now, the cost of living is more expensive, you know. In the early days things were very very cheap, you know, foodstuff and even all things from fish everything was cheap.

Harry: Am sure you have some things you remembered from when you were a child and when you were growing up, (is there) anything that stands out that you want to share, any cherished memories that you want to share with us?

Deane: When I grew up, I started to work and so, I didn't have any idle time. I work on a little land, you know, I planted the garden, and everything until I started out and at that time bananas hadn't come to the Island yet. When bananas production commenced in St. Vincent, I started to plant bananas also. The banana was a "terrible" (big) crop on the Island.

Harry: Not everything would have been smooth growing up, you would have had some challenges, some things in life that made life harder for you, do you recall any of those things, any challenges, any hardships that you faced growing up, whether as a child or when you became a big man?

Deane: No, I didn't feel any real hardship. The only hardship was one time I wasn't feeling so well. I was feeling sick and my father took me to the doctor in the hospital. He was a doctor named Gunmunro and when Gunmunro checked me, he said that I have hookworm and he gave me one medicine, one draught and I got rid of them and I got better.

Harry: And since then you are well?

Deane: Yes.

Harry: Ok, that's good. So, looking back on your lifetime, you're in your eighties now, if you were to change anything during that lifetime, what would you change? If there was something that you look back on now and say maybe I should have done it differently, any of those?

Deane: No, I don't have any regrets, because you know, I believe, you hear, in one God and He joined everything, He knows everything.

Harry: So, no regrets. If you have to live it over, you'll do it the same way you did?

Deane: Yes, I put everything, all my trust in God because He spared (my life) and I live up to this time. And all I have to do is serve Him in the right way. No turn back.

Harry: In terms of where we live, St, Vincent and the Grenadines, have you ever heard about the SVG Indian Heritage Foundation?

Deane: Yes, I heard about it. They used to have (meetings), but I never checked to go (to) all those places down there, Argyle down there.

Harry: Is that when they had the events in Argyle?

Deane: Yes.

Harry: So, you never got to attend any of the functions?

Deane: No, I didn't. I only see them on TV.

Harry: So you see it on the TV and maybe in the newspapers and otherwise?

Deane: Yes, mostly on the TV I see all those things because you know Harriet always used to be in all those things too you know. Harriet Deane.

Harry: Ok. Well, since you know about the organisation and the fact that we represent the persons of Indian descent who live in St. Vincent and the Grenadines, what would you like to see the organisation do for the people or accomplished for the people of St. Vincent and the Grenadines of Indian descent?

Deane: Well, according to the conditions I hear, they (are) doing very good because they remember the Indians.

Harry: So, did you enjoy the chat and sharing with us today?

Deane: Yes,

Harry: And thanks for taking the time to sit down and chat with me.

Commentary on interview with Mr Samuel Deane

The interview with Mr Samuel Deane corroborates many aspects given in the first two interviews by Mr Walter Bacchus and Mrs Theresa Jack. Like Mr Walter Bacchus' father, who moved from the Argyle estate to Chapel Yard then bought five acres of land at Glenside, his father also moved from the Argyle Estate to Peruvian Vale, then bought a large piece of land at Akers. During the next generations, their land was subdivided among their children, each getting smaller plots. Most of Mr Deane's aunts, uncles and siblings also migrated to the USA and Europe. There was also a transition in careers after indentureship. His dad was a farmer and tailor and Samuel continued in farming and also ventured out into trafficking to the Grenadines then to Trinidad. However, in the first and second generations after Indentureship, women were the primary caregivers for children and were responsible for managing the home, although some also worked as seamstresses and in retail.

On the right is one of those rare pictures in St. Vincent of an Indentured couple. They are the grandparents of Mr Samuel Deane. He is Mr William Deane who travelled on the ship, the Lightning in 1880 from India. His Indian name was Kalloo and his wife was Mary Deane. Other family members have said her Indian name was Puti Madhu.

Mr Deane's story about their journey and landing is however slightly different than the ship records. The ship records show that Kalloo came with his father, Ramphul, mother Anopia and younger sister, Bhugmonti. However, he was recorded as being only 9 years old and not 12 years as Mr Samuel Deane said he was told. He also said that Mary Deane came from Madras. The only ship that came from Madras to St. Vincent was the first ship, the Travancore in 1861, nineteen years earlier. The name Madhu does not seem to be within the records of any ship that came to St. Vincent. Even if Mary (Madhu) was one of the two babies that were born onboard the Travancore, Kalloo would have been ten years younger than her, which would be quite interesting as at that time Indian men generally married younger brides.

The story of the Lightning first landing in the Indian Bay area corresponds with the accounts of other elders, although the records show that all ships from India to St. Vincent landed at Edinboro in the Kingstown bay. Some Indians have claimed that Indian Bay beach was so named because the Indians from India landed there but this is disputed.

Trade, manufacturing and other businesses

Some Indians were also involved in a vibrant trade between St. Vincent and Trinidad, exporting livestock and agricultural produce to Trinidad and importing various other items. This trade continued into the 1960s and beyond. I remember, as a young child, seeing my uncle Percival (Val) Joseph, heading to Kingstown wharf with flocks of sheep and goats to be shipped to Trinidad. I also remember an older relative Mr Donald Woods importing and distributing the Madras brand of curry and concentrated essence from Trinidad. I even got involved in this trade when I lived in Trinidad in the 1980s, exporting hacksaw blades, hair accessories and other products to St. Vincent which my family distributed to retail shops in St. Vincent.

Several of the Indians in St. Vincent operated retail shops in places such as Georgetown, Park Hill, Richland Park, Calder, Rose Bank, Rose Hall and Kingstown. Three of the earliest people to establish shops in Richland Park were my grandmother, Alice Bacchus, her brother in law Mr Norman Bacchus and Mr Glaston Woods. Other Indians who operated grocery shops in Richland Park included Mrs Mega Ottley, Mr Gerald Bacchus, my father, Mr Alban Thomas, Mrs Marie Woods, Mrs Cecilia Thomas and Mrs Eucina Mounsey. The Indians therefore made a living and played a vital role by supplying food in some villages of St. Vincent.

The shop of Mrs Alice Bacchus, my grandmother, did not only distribute groceries but was also the purchasing point for nutmegs from local farmers. She would have the mace and nuts dried and processed and exported to Connecticut in the USA. My parents who opened their shop some years later continued this business but sold the dried mace and nuts to local exporters Mr Augustus "Chippy" Browne and Mr Dodds DaSilva of Mesopotamia.

Mrs Alice Bacchus also operated one of the first transport buses, Reliance, from Richland Park to Kingstown, the capital of St. Vincent. Her husband Mr Joseph Bacchus had done two work assignments in Aruba and like other Indians returned to St. Vincent and used the funds gained abroad to invest in property or businesses. Indians in other areas such as Georgetown and Rose Bank are also known to have operated transportation businesses.

The Indians were and are a resilient and entrepreneuring people and they survived and made a good living by a diverse form of activities, another of which was fish distribution. Two Indian businessmen from Richland Park, Mr Philbert (Filly) Thomas and Mr Gladstone Woods were distributors of fresh fish in the village. They would often obtain fresh fish from the seine pulled in the early hours of the morning on the Leeward side of the Island which they would retail in the village calling buyers by the blowing of the conch shell. Other of their relatives such as Mr Lloyd Bacchus were also in the fish business in other parts of the Island.

The Indians were also skilled in farming. Those in the dryer, seaside areas of the Island such as Argyle and Calder planted crops such as ground nuts (peanuts), sweet potatoes and corn, whereas those in the interior of the Island where there was more rainfall planted ground provisions such as yams, eddoes, dasheen and tannias. Cassava and vegetables were planted in diverse areas as they survived almost everywhere. They also had tree crops such as mangoes and livestock such as cattle and goats. Some of the plants and trees may have been offspring of plants brought from India.

Many Indians were involved in the cultivation of bananas after its introduction in St. Vincent. One visionary Indian of note who had made a significant contribution to the banana industry in St. Vincent was Mr Donelly Bacchus of Richland Park. Around 1952, when the St. Vincent Banana Growers was just being formed with funding from Mr Van Geeste of the UK, he along with others such as Mr S.O. Jack and Mr R. E. Baynes was intimately involved with the first program to produce bananas on a commercial scale in St. Vincent.

Mr Bacchus, along with my father, Alban Thomas, were few of the first to plant the imported Cavendish banana suckers (plants) at Simpson, Montreal, Richland Park. As the production of bananas increased in SVG, farmers were faced with the problem of a fungal disease, locally referred to as pin spot. Mr Bacchus came up with the idea of covering the bunch of bananas with plastic tubing and asked one of his workers, Mr Warren, to do so. The result was a success and this practice spread to other parts of SVG, and later globally.

As the banana industry grew in SVG, Mr Bacchus was the first to initiate the formation of rural boxing plants in SVG and subsequently established, with other farmers of the Indian community, the Kelly Par Boxing Plant, the first in SVG. At these plants the bananas were bought from farmers, graded, washed, boxed and sent in pallets to the ship to be exported to the UK. This boxing plant was later replicated throughout SVG.

There were other production processes and businesses that the Indians of Richland Park were involved with. These include the sewing and sale of caps, the production of soap blocks and their sale and export to nearby Caribbean Islands such as Grenada, St. Lucia and Trinidad. One business of significance in St. Vincent, which had its roots in sewing in the Richland Park community, is that of Mr Donelly Bacchus' sister Theresa and her husband Mr Nathaniel Jack.

They had learnt the hat making business from the family but diversified and later specialised in making school uniforms. They started with a few sewing machines on the ground floor of their house in Richland Park, then were later able to purchase the biggest business building (formerly P.H Viera supermarket) in Richland Park where they expanded the production business on the second floor and operated a store and supermarket on the top floor. Later, they expanded further into retail in Kingstown and also moved their production to the top floor there. They were later able to purchase another building in Kingstown from which Jax Enterprises is now one of the most dynamic businesses in the town. This story is similar to that of Mr Ormand and Aliena Baptiste of Calder who also specialize in clothing.

There were also other businesses in other parts of St. Vincent operated by Indians. These include the making of leather bags and purses by Mr Maurice Kydd, the making of caps by Mrs Edith Thomas neé Woods, Mr Owen Bacchus, Mr Alban Thomas, Mr Reynold Bowman and others. Mr Reynold Bowman of Richland Park as well as Mr Timon Woods' brother from Georgetown were also tailors. Mr Das Da Silva is another outstanding businessman of Indian descent who operates in Kingstown. He is famous for his black wine at Christmas time and his son Mr Kenneth DaSilva's brand Mountain Top is now a household name in St. Vincent. Several Indians also operated and some currently run pharmacies in Kingstown.

CHAPTER 7

Interview with Mrs Elise Williams

Williams: My name is Elise Williams. My father died when I was very young so I didn't even get to go to school but I could still read a little bit, you know. My father died when I was only fourteen and a half years (old). My father was Wilson Thomas and he died when he was 37 years (old). My mother was Elmina (Bacchus) Thomas and she came from Richland Park. She died when she was 72 (years old). All my family are mostly (from) Richland Park. Well, most are all gone, dead out. So, I don't have a large family.

Harry: So, were you born in Richland Park?

Williams: No, no, I (was) born at, you might not know those places, name Jack Gutter, that is down, yonder. My father had built a house down there. I (was) born down there.

Harry: Jack Gutter, you said, is that close to Akers?

Williams: Yes. I live in Calder now. I have lived here for about 40 (or) 50 years now, since I have been at this spot here.

Harry: Ok. What about your brothers and sisters?

Williams: Well, I had four brothers and four sisters and only one died. Do you want to know their names?

Harry: Yes, please.

Williams: I am the first one. My name is Elise Williams and I have a sister named Anita. Well, she is married (to a) Kydd and her name is Anita Kydd. And Teroy Thomas and Philix Thomas and Doreen Williams. She married Williams too. Cami, she died. And then Enos Thomas and Levi Thomas. So, those are all my sisters and brothers.

Harry: What about your children?

Williams: My children? I have five children and all of them (are) overseas. Two were just (visiting and) they just went back this month. So, they came to see me, two daughters and a granddaughter. Her name is Anesta Gaymes, that is the first one, and Inez Eastwood, that is her married name and Anette Bullock.

Harry: What about your immediate family, your uncles and aunts, (do) you remember their names on both sides, your mum and dad's sides?

Williams: I can't remember their names now.

Harry: What about your grandparents?

Williams: My grandparents, well, on my father's side, I can't remember his name, (if) it was Lily Thomas, something like that. And my mother's (mother), she came from Richland Park, I can't remember her name (Bhugmonti "Bunty" Rebecca Bacchus).

Harry: What about the other side of the family, do you remember that grandparents' names?

Williams: You mean on my father's side, no, I can't remember.

Harry: But do you know where they lived? Did they live in Calder or Akers or closeby?

Williams: Yes, they did live in Akers, over that side.

Harry: (Are there) any other relatives that you are close to, maybe a cousin or another close relative that you've been getting along with that you want to mention as well?

Williams: I can't remember their names but I grew up with all my family, and so, but around here, I don't really have any family, only neighbours, good neighbours, and so (on).

Harry: Did your parents or your grandparents ever tell you that their fore parents came from India? (Do you have) any stories about that?

Williams: No.

Harry: They didn't pass down any of that information, ok. So, besides your grandparents, you don't know much before that, they didn't mention much about that?

Williams: No, I don't remember.

Harry: What about life in earlier times when you were growing up, some of the things you remember when you were a little girl, into your teenage years and now as an adult. Tell me some of the things that you remember from those days.

Williams: I used to go with my dad to look after cattle and things.

Harry: You could tell me some of those stories, no problem, you can share those.

Williams: I used to go with him. He used to milk the cattle and give me the milk to bring up. Sometimes, I had to go with him to cut grass and so (on). You know in those days, children had to do a lot, and then come back. So, that's why I didn't get to go to school because he had to stay in the land to work. And then, when I go to school, I come back to carry his lunch, then make only half day school. And I used to go to a private school (where) we had to pay a penny a week. Hahaha, sometimes when I pass up to that end when I am going to town and I see the building, I do remember there I used to go to school. (It's) an old building when you are going up on this road.

Harry: Up in Calder itself?

Williams: Yes, yes, up, when you are going up Belmont. The old building is still there. So, when I (was a child) I had to walk from there and walk to Akers, you know. So much walking. And then, I had to go carry my father's lunch down (to) Argyle. So, by the time I come back, it's (already) late, I can't get back to school. That's why I didn't get a lot of education but praise God, I can still read my Bible and do everything. Yes, I practice by going to church and so (on).

Harry: So, when you grew up you had a lot of time in the lands helping your father.

Williams: Yes, with my father, helping my father.

Harry: How would you say life is different now from what you see compared to when you were growing up.

Williams: Well, I think life is easier now. I feel so for the children because some of the children these days don't even get up on time to go to school (but for us) we had to do so much work before we went to school. We had to bring water in a bucket.

Harry: So, life is easier for the children now? You don't have to carry water on your head.

Williams: Yes, life is easier. You go in the kitchen, water is there, you go outside, water is there.

Harry: And you don't have to go to the river to bathe and wash with your hand or dig potatoes before you go to school.

Williams: Yes, haha it's true. You had to wash with your hand but now you have machines, you just put all (your clothing) in there and wash. Praise God. You had to "droge" (carry) the wood on your head. Yes, since I live here I droge wood on my head because I didn't have any stove until I managed to buy a stove. So, it was really (more difficult) days. So, the children these days are so happy because they have everything.

Harry: (Is there) anything special you remembered about growing up, any treasured memories, any special times you wish to talk about?

Williams: Growing up in a poor home, in a very small (house), the first time when I just got married, I married when I was fifteen years old and when I first got married, it (was) in a little wattle house where I lived. In a little, little house over there. So, I lived there for a long time and came back and started this one. Then my husband went away (abroad to work) and we tried to finish it and that's it.

Harry: Ok. What was your husband's name though?

Williams: Hurious Williams.

Harry: Ok.

Williams: He died seven years ago.

Harry: So, you were living here before he passed (away)?

Williams: Yes, yes, yes.

Harry: Ok.

Williams: He died seven years (ago because) it will be seven in August.

Harry: So, you were married from when you were fifteen and how old was he, do you remember?

Williams: When did he die?

Harry: No, when you and he got married, about how old?

Williams: He was only sixteen. Sixteen or seventeen, something like that.

Harry: So you would have been married for well over sixty plus years when he passed away?

Williams: Yes, yes.

Harry: That's a very long time.

Williams: Yes, we lived a good life and a long life together.

Harry: If you were to change anything in your lifetime when you look back and see all that you did and some of the things you know, and some of the people you had around you and life in general, (is there) anything you would have liked to do differently or change?

Williams: I don't think so.

Harry: So, you feel as though you lived your life to the fullest and you enjoyed every bit of it, a fulfilling life?

Williams: "Uhu" (Yes)

Harry: As a country on a whole, looking at St. Vincent and the Grenadines, if you had a chance to change anything around you, the way we live, the way we get along, the way we relate to one another, what would that be?

Williams. I don't have anything that I feel could change because you can't change your neighbours, and I live well with them. I feel happy just like how I am. I just pray to God that he will keep me and guide me and protect me, comfort me and strengthen me. When the night comes, I go to sleep and in the morning I get up when I feel like getting up and that's it.

Harry: And you have good neighbours that look out for you, you said?

Williams: Yes. Well, if anything happens, I can call them and they can come and help but I must always say that God is my help in everything. In everything, God is my help.

Harry: (Have) you ever heard about the SVG Indian Heritage Foundation?

Williams: Yes, I heard about it and my daughter and my son-in-law used to attend that, something like that in town, and they used to have something like that in town?

Harry: Yes, and in Argyle and other places.

Williams: Yes, well then, they used to go and so on. I went once (to a function) at Argyle.

Harry: And how was that?

Williams: It was good.

Harry: (Did) you get to see some of the dancing and the cultural pieces?

Williams: No, I didn't see that.

Harry: In terms of the organisation itself, what would you like to see the organisation do, the fact that we represent the people of Indian descent who live in St. Vincent and the Grenadines, what do you think we can do to (improve) the relationship with the people and to reach out and make connections on behalf of the people?

Williams: I don't see anything else you could do. I don't have any knowledge of that, you see. I find everything is going alright. I don't know.

Harry: So, (is there) anything you would like to add before we wrap up, any stories you'd want to tell us that we didn't get before?

Williams: (No)

Harry: So, (did) you enjoy the little conversation we had?

Williams: Oh, yes.

Harry: (Did) you enjoy sharing it?

Williams: Yes

Harry: So, what we want to do now, what we recorded with you, we are going to prepare it, so we can share with others, so they can hear about your life growing up and so on. Is that ok with you?

Williams: Yes, yes.

Harry: All of this will come in to help others understand how connected we all are, how the family are related and so on. We appreciate you taking time to chat with us. Ok, thank you.

Williams: Thank you very much.

Commentary on interview with Mrs Elise Williams

Interconnections of the Indians in SVG

Mrs Elise Williams' family connections reveal an aspect of the Indians in St. Vincent that is quite unique. It is usually said that all of the Indians in St. Vincent and the Grenadines are related. Whereas this may be a slight exaggeration, it is highly likely that almost all of the Indians from SVG are related in one way or the other. Mrs Williams' family for example is connected to the Wilson,

Bacchus and Deanes which are in turn also connected to many other families. This is mainly due to the fact that although those who came from India may not have been related and came from different towns, clans and religions, they abandoned those affiliations shortly after arriving in St. Vincent.

However, the second, third and fourth generations in SVG didn't generally marry people outside of the Indian race and Indians continued in SVG. Although the proportion of the population of Indians in other Caribbean Islands such as Jamaica, St. Lucia and Grenada were also relatively small, there were fewer marriages with other races in St. Vincent and the Grenadines. It is known that the Indian men in St. Vincent would even travel to other villages to find an Indian wife. They avoided marrying into other races. As one second generation Indian, Mr James (Chowbow) Woods puts it, "those marriages (usually) break up". In the villages of Richland Park and Calder for example, it was notable that about ninety percent of the Indian couples were of the same race. These marriages usually lasted for a lifetime, in the case of Mr and Mrs Williams over sixty years.

Notwithstanding the Indians surviving, there was more assimilation into the wider community when compared to Trinidad and Guyana. The sociologist would therefore classify St. Vincent and the Grenadines as a more plural society where the peoples of Indian, African, and European descent more readily adopted parts of each other's cultures to produce a melting pot with significantly less racial conflicts as occurred in Guyana and Trinidad.

Racial intermarriages are more common now in St. Vincent and the Grenadines. It is therefore quite correct to conclude that a significant amount of the 23% of the population who classified themselves in the 2012 census to be of "mixed" race would have some Indian heritage. Whereas all of the 1.1% (or about 1,200) of the population classified themselves Indians, this figure is quite small when compared to the 6% a few decades ago. This could be due mainly to racial assimilation and/or outward migration. As Mrs Williams confirmed, most of her family, including siblings and children, migrated abroad.

A simple, yet contented life

Mrs Williams pointed out that although she lived a simple life, she was generally satisfied with her achievements over the years. Although life was hard, she made decisions that were appropriate in the circumstances so that in her retirement years she had no regrets.

She grew up in a home that depended on farming. Like in many typical Indian families at the time, the children had to help in performing the day to day tasks such as carrying water, milk, lunch, firewood and sometimes working on the farm. In many cases, like hers, this affected their ability to obtain a primary and secondary school education.

They could not afford luxurious houses and as Mrs Williams stated, when she got married, she lived in a wattle and daub house. They were only able to build a concrete house after her husband went abroad to improve their economic situation. Several other Indians went to Aruba and returned in a better financial state but many who went to the United Kingdom and North America settled in those countries because of the better economic and educational opportunities available to them and their children.

Like Mrs Williams' family, those who remained in St. Vincent did whatever was possible to improve their financial situation. In her family's case they operated a grocery shop among other things. Their faith in God's guidance and care, as she stated, was important in steering a contented and satisfied life within their means.

CHAPTER 8

Interview with Mr Patrick Deane

Harry: Can you tell me your full name and your occupation please?

Deane: Patrick Deane, retired businessman.

Harry: And what was your former occupation?

Deane: Railwayman in England.

Harry: Ok. And how old are you now?

Deane: Next month, I'll be 75 (years old).

Harry: Ok, where do you currently live?

Deane: Since I came back from England, I set up my home here in Golden Vale but I lived before in Akers. I was born in Cane End.

Harry: What were your parents' names?

Deane: My father's name was Donald Deane of Akers, my mother's name was Veronica Da Silva. She was from Cane End. Silky and Star Garage people are my uncles. My mother was Da Silva. My father was a landowner. I think they called them peasant proprietors or something like that.

Harry: And, what about your brothers and sisters?

Deane: My brother, one, he passed away two years ago. He was the owner of Deane's Pharmacy. And I (and) my wife, what's her name again, we had Deane's Beauty Salon in Egmont Street. Most of the hairdressers and so on you're seeing now in St. Vincent are ex-employees of my wife. She revolutionized and she brought hairdressing here to St. Vincent. All this, with their ear rings in their ears and all (those) things, we brought them here. Jerry Curls, we brought that here. Weaving, she brought it here.

Harry: Do you have any uncles or aunts? What were their names?

Deane: Yes, many. Well, they have all died now but I grew up around them. Walter, that was my favourite uncle. As a little boy, I lived with him.

Harry: What's his surname?

Deane: Deane, all Deane. And then, there was Vincent. That's Sonny's father. There was Joseph. I don't think you would know those people. Sebastian Deane, Leonard Deane. That was their father. And Cheryl's dad, Jonathan. He died when I was very small but I remember him.

Harry: Was that the same one we refer to as Yambou Deane?

Deane: Yes. That's Cheryl's father. Right. And there were aunties. I remember some of them. There was Mrs George, Mrs Henry. Those are two aunties that I remembered. And there was one name Clara, Kathy and I forgot what the other one's name was. They (are) based in America. They went to America when I was a little fella but a couple of times, they visited home, especially Clara. I remember her very, very well. Nice woman! And Das DaSilva's wife. That's Carmen. We grew up as little kids together. I am trying to remember the name of her mother, you know. She died quite a few years (ago).

Harry: What about your grandparents, what do you know about them?

Deane: I have fond memories, especially of my grandmother because, to begin with, I never knew my mother.

Harry: (Do) you remember your grandparents on both sides of the family?

Deane: Yes, yes, I remember my grandparents. My father's father, it's a funny thing, they tried to break up the relationship between my father and my mother. My mother had two children for him, me and my brother. So, what they did, they took the two children away from my mother and they carried them up to Akers. That's how I ended up in Akers. But I was so small, I think I was probably about nine months old. I didn't know.

Harry: Ok

Deane: So, any person that hugged me, I was happy with that. So, my grandmother took me but my brother was a bit older and he cried all night, day and night for two days. So, they sent him back. So, I never knew I had a brother until I was about, maybe six years old. I never knew I had a brother. They kept us apart. But, it's a funny thing, you see. My grandfather loved me! The relationship that he wanted to break, you know what I mean, the child (me) he loved me, really, really loved me. He had an accident so he wasn't working anymore. He stayed in the house by a sofa. And I always had to be on the sofa with him, eating biscuits and chocolate and this and that with him. I was the apple of his eye. And I was to have taken over the lands. He had a good portion of land but I don't want to go into all that (detail).

Harry: That's ok.

Deane: They had a family squabble and things like that, right, and my grandmother, oh boy, my grandmother, anything I wanted I got from my grandmother, anything I wanted. I remember as a little kid, she had a little old woman (who) used to work with her and they used to boil starch to starch clothes and I used to go with a cup, I remember. I used to say grandma, grandma oh, (I want) some porridge. She (would) say alright Bo. Bo in Indian I think means son. She will say, you can't eat this, I will make you some. And she would leave the other old woman to do the clothes and she would take me in the kitchen and she would make arrowroot, we called it pop, arrowroot pop for me and she would sit down with me and cool it and give it to me. She was just a wonderful old lady. Just a wonderful, wonderful, wonderful old lady. Anytime I speak about her, it brings something to my throat. I still love that woman. I loved that woman.

Harry: Did they ever tell you about their family from India?

Deane: I didn't get much from them about their families in India. At one time, I think they went to try to live in Trinidad but they didn't like it, so they came back to St. Vincent. My grandfather worked on the Argyle estate and he used to get halfpenny a day to clean out, he was about ten years old and he used to clean out the stables. And he worked his way, the first thing he did was to try to learn English. That's the first thing he did, try. He spoke with an accent but he knew English very well and he could read, write and count. And he told me, he said, he reared animals in (the) Argyle river. And out of whatever he did, when the estate was being sold out, he became something like a ganger. On the estate they planted cotton in those days, so he had a gang of workers.

Harry: Like how you have road gangs now cleaning the road.

Deane: Yes, He was a ganger and he rode a mule. Hahaha and he was proud of that. And when they were selling out the estate, (as) the owner was going back to England, he asked him. He said, (do) you have any money? So, he said yes. In those days you had a few guineas. It was 21 shillings in those days. It was a pound, shilling and pence. So, a guinea was 21 shillings. Ok, so you learn that eh, a guinea was 21 shillings. So, he told the guy he had whatever, how much guineas he had. So, he asked him, would you like a piece of land? So, he told him, yes. So he said where do you want it? He said, I knew Akers was flat land but it was covered with trees and what's the name. So, he carried him up there and showed him, and he said, I'd like a piece of this. In those days they didn't have surveyors, they had lineman with a ball of twine and a few knots inside of it. So, they went up to Akers and I think he was able to get ten acres.

Harry: Wow, that's a lot of land.

Deane: That's plenty of land. And, then he gave him a piece of wooded land for nothing. He said, there you are, that piece over there, have that for your wood, to make firewood or if you want to build anything. He said, right. So, he took that off him. And (he took) a lot of the guys, the Indian guys who came over to work as indentured workers, up to to Akers and the first thing he did was (to) build a long room and put them inside it. Because these guys were not married. They had no wives.

Harry: Like an apartment, a little apartment complex.

Deane: Well, you know, they throw themselves down anyway. And he made sure they had food and things but he said some of them used to drink and he couldn't take that. So, he had a gang, the same sort of gang he had with him and he used them to clean the lands up. And then he put his first crop of cotton in. That's what he told me. I remember those stories. I'll tell you something. He told me how hard they had to work on the estate. They had ploughs, they had ploughs and one day they had an Indian thing at Argyle. I went there and they had a plough and I walked up and I held on to that plough. Tears run down my eyes when I remember my grandfather. He told me about the plough, how hard (they had to work).

Harry: And he probably used that very plough.

Deane. In the sun, they had to work. Not just him but the other guys. They had to work and they had to (do) things with this plough in the blazing sun. And they were told that they were coming to St. Vincent and after a certain time they will go back, they will make money and go back and none of them ever went back. And none of them ever got any money. And these people, they sort of capitalize on them for nothing. And I went up to that plough and I held on to the handle and I remembered my grandfather.

Harry: Did he ever tell you where he was from in India?

Deane: I can't remember too well where he said he was from. My grandmother was from Calcutta. She was very light skinned. I don't know what tribe she was (from) but she was very light-skinned. But my grandfather was a dark, tall fellow, six feet plus, a very tall fellow. One of my sons looks nearly like him. Very, very tall fellow. Well, he used to play cricket, my grandfather.

Harry: Oh, he was a cricketer?

Deane: Yes, he used to play cricket with the white guys on the estate. (Is) there a place named Punjab?

Harry: Punjab province, yes.

Deane: I think that's where he was from. I am not too sure but I think that's where he was from. Possibly. But my grandmother came from Calcutta. She lived at Tourama, I don't know how she got up there, up on the Windward side.

Harry: That is close to the Geothermal area up there.

Deane: Yes, Tourama. That's where she came from.

Harry: That's close to Lot 14.

Deane: I don't know St. Vincent all that well. At one time she had either fourteen or sixteen children alive hahaha but most of them are away, plenty went off to America.

Harry: Where did most of your family live? Was it concentrated in the Calder, Argyle area or scattered in different areas?

Deane: Yes, yes, Calder.

Harry: Akers, those areas, close to the Argyle estate.

Deane: Yes. Well, I think the Argyle estate. They had big houses, big accommodations for them. So they lived there, right. And my grandmother told me that they had a disease that took a lot of them.

Harry: Was it cholera? Cholera passed through in the 1800s.

Deane: Yes, yes. My grandmother told me about that.

Harry: There is a burial ground near the Convent school in Kingstown.

Deane: She even gave me a story. She said the guy who used to bury them was a fella named Spence. He was the man that used to take their corpses away and bury them. The Indians in those days used to have lots of gold trinkets on their hands. She said there was a lady (who had) lots of gold trinkets on her hand, rings and so on. Well this woman wasn't dead. So, Spence got his guys organised and they carried her and put her in a trench but she wasn't dead. And then later on in the night, he went there to pull the jewellery off her hand and she grabbed hold of his hand. Hahaha.

Harry: I understand they used to bury people alive.

Deane: Yeah, but he knew that she was not dead, so he laid her in the trench and left her there, then he went back in the night to get the things off her hand and she grabbed onto his hand and wouldn't let go. That's a death hold. Haha. They heard Spence down there bawling. Haha, So the fellers took lamps and went down hahaha and they nearly killed Spence. My grandmother told me about that. The woman held on to Spence's hand and no matter how much he tried to get away (he couldn't).

Harry: She had the Cholera too?

Deane: Yeah, but that is the death hold. You come to bury me, you come thief.

Harry: That was probably in the 1860s or thereabout (X1890s)

Deane: Yeah, somewhere around there because both my grandfather and grandmother, you know, (lived long). My grandfather was a hundred and something plus when he died and I watched him die. I was a little fellow, I didn't know what was going on.

Harry: So he was born in the 1800s?

Deane: Yeah, it got to be (so). He kept saying, when he came to St. Vincent, he was around ten (X9) years old and when he died, he was well over a hundred and something years old. And he died with all his marbles. He wasn't stupid or anything. I watched him die. As a little kid, I followed my grandmother up and down. Everywhere she goes, I am behind my grandmother. Everywhere she goes. So, she was sitting on the bed with my grandfather and they spoke Hindi. I know a little bit of it. Maybe if I stayed with them long enough, I would have picked it up. And my grandfather was speaking to my grandmother and he said something to her. But I remember, he asked her for water and though I couldn't speak the language, I knew a lot of the words. My grandfather said to my grandmother paanee, and paanee is water. So, my uncle was at the front of the house. You have (a) hall and chamber. He was up to the front. Maybe he was reading or something. So, my grandmother called my uncle and said, "Walter, bring a glass with some water and bring a spoon". (In) less than a few seconds, Walter (came). There wasn't pipe water, water was in a goblet. (Do) you know what a goblet is? It's made from clay and keeps water very cool and nice, right? So, he came with it and my grandmother took her husband's head and put it in her lap. Walter came with the spoon and he, my grandfather, opened his eyes like this and he watched and he opened his mouth like this and Walter gave him a spoonful of water. He drank it and took another. And all I remembered I saw was a big bubble of air coming up from his mouth. Big bubble. He was dead, you know.

Harry: Ok.

Deane: Well, I didn't know he died. Just a big air bubble came up from my grandfather's mouth and his head just went like that. After he drank the first spoonful of water, he looked at my grandmother and he had a big smile on his face. He didn't speak but he had a big smile like he was laughing or something, right? And when they gave him the second thing of water, he just did his head (so) and a big bubble of air came out. And my grandmother started to cry. She held him and she was saying either Bapu or Babu. It's an Indian word, Babu. And she started to cry and she held him in her arms like that. And she started to cry. And I (as) a little fella, I didn't know what was happening but my grandmother was crying so I started to cry too. Then, my uncle held his mother and he said alright, alright, alright. And they got something and they tied his jaw up like that. He didn't have any teeth so he tied his jaw up like that and got something and tied his two (big) toes together, straightened his feet and tied his two toes together. And I keep crying because my grandmother was crying but they won't tell me what happened to Babu. They would not tell me. So, my father was in an old house further down, like a storeroom, that's where he used to stay. So, Walter ran down there and called him and he came up. And then there was a funeral arrangement and all that and they buried him in the Catholic church. Oh, I think it's the day before he died, the Catholic minister came up and gave him his communion. He used to come regularly. He was a Hindu but Catholic you know. He was a very learned man, a very learned man. He had lots and lots of Indian books and he sent them down to Argyle between the fresh and the salt and let them go.

Harry: Ok.

Deane: It was his beliefs, you know, what he believed in. He was a wonderful man, wonderful, wonderful man.

Harry: Well, you mentioned your uncle, (were there) any of the other relatives that you remember, other than your grandparents?

Deane: Yes, I remember as I said when Yambou Deane died. I remember going to his funeral. There was Sebastian Deane, he at one time had a big shop in Calder. Sebastian's father was my uncle. That's my father's brother. His name was Joseph and they used to call him Willie Deane. He was a nice man, a very nice man. I remember him. Everytime he came he would give me one of those "Extra Strong" hahaha and I had to run to get water, a cup of water. Everytime he came, my father used to tell him, don't give the boy those things, (they) burn up his mouth. Oh ho ho ho, that's good for him, keep him something or the other. I remember him, his name was Willie. Uncle Willie, haha, that was Sebastian's father. Sonny's dad was a tailor. He used to make trousers and so on so they called him Tailor Deane.

Harry: I heard that name before. As it pertains to you, what do you remember about your earlier times growing up, your teenage years and some of the things you remember most about those times?

Deane: Well, I remember being very lonely. That's one thing I remember, I remember being very lonely growing up as a little boy. I didn't have any toys to play with. I didn't have another little child or fella to play with. Not until I met my brother who must have been about eight or nine years old and I discovered I had a brother. Our days together were very enjoyable but very short because I went away. I think I spent eight or nine years with them, then I went off to England. My mother was a wonderful lady. She taught me and my brother to sing and do harmonies and so on. My brother and I used to sing. And then I went off to England. I used to sing up there. I used to sing in Pubs and so on. I made a few dollars out of it but I got married very very young. I think I was twenty when I got married. I don't think it spoiled my opportunities but I took responsibility (as) I had a young wife with a kid and things like that, not like today. Today you get the chance to go to school, to go to any place. You know, people knock the Trade Unions but the Trade Unions change a lot of things and open up opportunities for lots of people. So, I was just like any ordinary kid. There weren't many places to go. You had to find your own entertainment. So my mother, my brother and I, three of us used to get together and we used to sing. My brother could play a nice guitar. I used to play a cuatro. The guitar inside there. We made our own entertainment. And the youngsters around in the village were very helpful. Not like today. The youngsters were very helpful. Many times, we have something to do, two, three, four youngsters will come along and help me and my brother. Give us a pull out you know. And we helped each other, very loving to one another. And I loved that.

Harry: Would you say life is different now, how people live, how people get along?

Deane: Oh, yeah, people don't seem to have much time for one another today. The children today, (if) you pass down the street and a young boy sees you he doesn't say anything to you. He just looks, he doesn't even look at you, he just walks past you. You couldn't do that in my time. So, (if you see) a lady or a gentleman, whether you know him or not, you have to say good morning sir (or) good morning madam. If you didn't do it and he knew your father or your mother, he would complain. Your mother will probably call you and grab you and give you two clouts and say "you passed Mr Crick on the road yesterday, why didn't you speak to him?" (You could) find some excuse but you will get a clout hahaha.

Harry: You would have had some treasured memories growing up, what stands out most in terms of those, some of the most memorable moments for you growing up?

Deane: There was a school concert in Evesham and I sang there and Mr Latham was the local representative, Levi latham. And the headmistress called on him to move a congratulatory (message) to the scholars and the parents and he held the microphone in his hand and he started to tremble. I felt sorry for him hahaha. There was a guy who lived next to the school's boundary and we used to play cricket there and we had a stone, a big stone up in the air like that. That was the wicket. So when you bowl, sometimes the breadfruit or the orange ball used to go over in his banana field and he used to stay there with a cutlass and cut them up. One day he cut his foot hahaha. The cutlass cut his foot and everybody started laughing hahaha.

Harry: Through all of that you must have had some difficult times, (is there) any in particular that stands out, any hardships, any particular thing, that you struggled with?

Deane: I will say this to you, but it's no reflection really because looking at it today and times changed. I had problems in school with kids of different races. I used to like to play marbles. When I went and played with the Indian kids, they used to chase me. They (are not) playing with stinking skin creole and that kind of rubbish. And when I went and played with them, (the creoles), they (were not playing) with licey head C. So, I turned out to be a fighter. I learned to fight. I put my marble down and I say if you are not going to play with me, who (is) not going to play with me, bang (slap) or I pick a stone and I pelt it. My brother and I (hahaha) learned to fight. We (never) used to skylark, we learned to fight. You're going to play with me or nobody plays here today. I put my marble down, and I say, you playing with me, or nobody playing here and I have a stone in my pocket.

Harry: If you had a chance to change something in your life, when you're looking back now, what would that be? (Is there) anything in particular that you would do differently?

Deane: No, no, not really, not really. How things are today, especially from an educational standpoint, it's wonderful, I wish I had that opportunity. Long time (days) if your father or mother or somebody couldn't send you to school and pay your school fees and pay your transportation and (give you) some money to get something to eat, you couldn't (get an education). No matter how light your head was, you couldn't get to secondary school to get a secondary education. I was fortunate, I got some but I didn't complete school. I reached Form 4. And whatever I got, it made a great, great difference to my life when I went to England. It made a great difference to me. It wasn't completed but it was enough for me to work my way up on the railway.

Harry: Now, from a country standpoint, if you had an opportunity to change certain things about the way we get along, the way people relate, SVG on a whole, what would you do?

Deane: Well, I have a problem with men as a whole. They go along and they make children and they do not take up their responsibility. That is something that worries me. Us kind of people (Indians) mostly take our responsibility seriously but there are some guys out there, they don't care, they pull up their pants and walk off. And those fellas, if I ever had the opportunity to be Prime Minister or whatever, I will pass a law. Any woman who could come to the family court and bring a guy and say, this guy is the father of my child, I don't care what he say, it could be ten men that you been with, ten of you will mind that child until you go to court and get a DNA test and prove, you have to do it, prove that the child is not yours. Because every child out there has a father. And all they do is just bring problems into society. That's what they do, bring problems into society. And most of the children that get themselves in trouble come from a broken home. No father, no father, that's the problem we have. And that is a problem for me. You father a child, mind your child. Mind your child, that is one thing that is (unacceptable) to me. You see a woman, she has three children, one in her arms here, one there, she is going down the road, where is the father? Where are they?

Harry: As it relates to the SVG Indian Heritage Foundation, do you know about the Indian Heritage Foundation? If so, what do you know about it?

Deane: Well, when it first started, I used to go, I probably went about two, three times.

Harry: What would you like to see the organisation accomplish?

Deane: I don't know what their long term-plan is. What have they got? What is the future of it? I noticed they are trying to link up with India which to me is the right direction because India has so much to offer. From an educational (viewpoint), India has so much to offer. So much. And what about the Indians, don't they have Indians in Grenada?

Harry: I believe they do but am not sure if they have an organisation there.

Deane: Well, maybe if they don't have an organisation, we can feel out and reach out to them because we are all one people. We are all one people. They have Indians in St. Lucia, they have Indians in Barbados, they have Indians all over the Caribbean. Lots of Indians in Trinidad.

Harry: Well, Trinidad has their own establishment in terms of a fully function-ing organisation.

Deane: Well, all right, maybe we should try to link up with them and learn from them.

Harry: Well, our connection (to India) is actually through Suriname. Our Ambassador is based in Suriname. Through him, we are in contact with India. We can't connect directly with India unless we go through the Ambassador who is in charge. We are in touch with India through our Ambassador.

Deane: Whatever it is, we have to stretch our hands out and link our hands together. We are all one people. If I tell you, Ken Thomas down the road is my cousin. Roberts, Ken Thomas' sister, is my cousin. All the Bacchus up in Richland park are my cousins, everyone of them are my cousins. In Calder, all the Thomases, all of them, you will be surprised, they were my grandfather's brothers and sisters. They are all one people and then they intermarry with one another, so we all become one melting pot. Dr Lewis, the dental (specialist) is related. We are related, all related. All the Indians are related. You check it, the Sutherlands in Georgetown, they are related, the Pereiras are related. My best friend in England, James Pereira, (was also known as) Bruds Pereira. His aunty was married to De Caul. (Do) you know Decaul from Calder? Decaul and my mother are related on the Da Silva side. Ferrari, on my mother's side, are all related. You know, if you check the whole human race, somewhere we are related. Well, that's what I would like to see, we stretch our hands across the water and unite. Unite the Indians. Don't bother with those other people, they always drink and misbehave.

Harry: Ok. Well, I think that is about it. I hope you enjoy the little exchange and communication.

Deane: Yes, wonderful.

Harry: (Did) you enjoy sharing the stories?

Deane: Yes, yes. Some of it I have forgotten.

Harry. I understand. That's ok. Over the years certain things may slip you. So let me just thank you. Thanks a lot.

Commentary on interview with Mr Patrick Deane

Introduction

The information gathered from Mr Patrick Deane was quite revealing and confirmed the narratives of other elders. His family demonstrated upward mobility in educational achievements, careers and economic well being. From farming, they moved into areas such as tailoring, shop ownership and dentistry. There was one difference between him and Mr Samuel Deane's interview regarding the origin of their grandmother (Madhu Puti) Mary Deane. He said she was from Calcutta rather than Madras. This is still to be verified as we have not yet identified her name on the ship lists. However, Mr Patrick Deane gave a fuller description of various topics including life on the estate for the indentured workers, land acquisition, relinquishing Indian traditions, racial assimilation and life for the second and third generation of Indian children.

Life on the estates

Mr Deane confirmed that life for his grandfather on the Argyle estate was very rough and difficult. He had to work hard, even at the age of ten to clean the horse stables and later worked in the fields in "the blazing sun" for very little wages. The indentured workers were disappointed that they were not able to obtain the amount of wages promised before they left India and many of them were not able to save any or much money.

It was interesting to note that Mr Deane's grandfather was able to save some guineas. He also learnt English and how to count and read etc. He played cricket with the white planters and overseers. There therefore was some enjoyment notwithstanding the difficulties faced.

Land Acquisition

Mr Deane's grandfather was able to buy ten 10 acres of land. The estate owner appeared to be very generous and helpful in giving him extra wooded lands. There are similar stories where faithful or hardworking Indians were given good deals to purchase lands. One Indian, Mr James Morgan, got over 80 acres of wooded land in Montreal, at Gaskill on the western side of the Petit Bonhomme mountain.

Giving up Traditions

The story of the woman who died during the cholera outbreak highlighted the fact that a lot of jewellery was still worn by Indian women by the end of the 1800s. However, this tradition has declined possibly because of acculturation and getting accustomed to Christian values among other things. Mr Deane's grandfather was a learned man who studied lots of Hindu books but threw these into the sea, at the river mouth between the "salt and the fresh" and became a Catholic. This change in culture and traditions was also seen in Mr Deane and his brother playing the guitar and cuatro rather than traditional Indian instruments.

Racial Assimilation

Mr Patrick Deane's experiences as a child of mixed race shows how the different races in St. Vincent and the Grenadines dealt with each other and how their stance has softened generally over the years. This does not mean that there isn't any racism in the country but it is generally not as pronounced or overt as before or as in other Caribbean territories such as Guyana and Trinidad.

As a child with some African and Indian genes, he was scoffed at by the children of both African and Indian descent. Children of both races didn't want to play marbles with him. Having grown up as a young child with his Indian grandparents he felt the love they had for him. He also felt the love of his mother in his teenage years who was of another race. So, the attitude of his schoolmates must have been baffling, hence as he said he became a fighter. Whereas both the Indian and African sides of his family loved him, this love may not have been shown by these same people to other races. The fact that he was taken by his grandparents showed there was some racial tension. The great thing was that he won their hearts even if they may have had different attitudes before.

These types of relationships between Indians and people of other races would have contributed to the relatively faster racial assimilation in the smaller Islands of the Caribbean. However, racism still exists as noted by another elder, Mr Winston Bacchus who mentioned the subtle racism that was practiced when he was selected to pursue further education in Barbados. Many Indians were highly motivated to achieve higher levels of education and economic wellbeing. When compared to other races in St. Vincent, they were generally relatively very successful.

Life for Second and Third Generation Indians

Most of the interviewees in this edition were second or third generation of those who travelled from India to St. Vincent. Either their grandparents or great grandparents were former citizens of India. For example, Mr Patrick Deane and Mr Samuel Deane's grandparents were Indian immigrants and Mrs Theresa Jack's grandparents and great grandparents were from India. These generations had a much different life than the indentured workers and the current generations.

Whereas the first generation suffered life threatening diseases such as cholera, these seem to have faded away by the second and third generations. This may be due to the availability of better health services. The second and third generations had cases of less severe diseases such as yaws, trigger and hookworm, but these are now non-existent in St. Vincent. However, it is paradoxical that many

Indians of the previous generations lived longer lives, some over one hundred years. Could this be attributed to hard work and a diet with less meat?

Sports were being developed during the time of the older generations albeit with makeshift gears such as cricket balls being improvisations of young oranges and breadfruit. Now children have better sporting gear and toys. One thing that this older generation of children were better at, as Mr Patrick Deane pointed out, was that they had better manners and respect. In the olden days a child couldn't pass an adult without greeting them by saying good morning etc. As the Vincentian society becomes more developed this culture is changing.

CHAPTER 9

Interview with Mr Noel Soleyn

Harry: Can you give me your full name and occupation please?

Soleyn: Noel Adolph Soleyn.

Harry: Ok, where do you currently reside?

Soleyn: Rosebank.

Harry: Your parents, what were their names and occupations, what did they do?

Soleyn: My mother was a homemaker and my father was a labourer. He did all kinds of odd jobs. He did farming, mostly but he would migrate every now and again to England where he would make some money and come home because he didn't want to leave his children alone. So he (would) do two years and come home and maybe spend four years (with the family) and then go back again and come again. So that's about the long and short of that. My mum had eleven children, so she couldn't do any work anywhere else.

Harry: By the way, how old are you now?

Soleyn: I'll be 65 this year.

Harry: What about your brothers and your sisters? Do you have any brothers and sisters?

Soleyn: Oh, yeah. There were eleven of us in the family. One just died, he would be buried today in Corpus Christi, Texas.

Harry: Ok, what are their names?

Soleyn: There is Kenneth, Edward, Kathy, Clayton, he is dead, Patricia, Sam, Ingrid, I, of course, Paul, Susie and Julie.

Harry: And they're all scattered in different places?

Soleyn: The majority of them are in the United States.

Harry: Ok

Soleyn: Kenny is in England and the rest of us (are) at home. Three of us are at home (in SVG). Patricia, Susie and I.

Harry: What about your uncles and aunts, those on both sides?

Soleyn: There is one uncle left alive. He lives in Florida. All the others are dead. But I had on my mother's side, one aunt and one uncle because there were three of them. On my father's side, we had uncle John, uncle Joe, uncle William, aunty Jeana, two other aunts. One was Tanty Meena and one was Mrs Crosby.

Harry: Those are those that you are aware of?

Soleyn: Yes, on my father's side.

Harry: Your grandparents, (do) you know anything about them?

Soleyn: My grandfather used to live at Chilli.

Harry: That's in Georgetown?

Soleyn: Yes, he was there at a place he called, I remember him telling me he was at Lot 14 in the eruption.

Harry: Ah, that's where the Geothermal site is sitting now or there about.

Soleyn: But he said that the avalanche came down and covered parts of Lot 14 and he said a lot of people were scalded to death. His mother was one of them who died in (the) 1902 eruption. He was born here but my great grandfather on my mother's side was Bharatt Singh. He came here in 1862. He came on the boat lift in 1862 and when he was christened in 1875, they changed his name from Bharatt Singh to James Alexander because one of their godparents' names was James Alexander.

Harry: And in those days they gave you your godparents' surname.

Soleyn: Just like his other relatives over here. Well, he wasn't his relative but he was married to his sister. His name was George Bones. That was the name of the priest who christened him in the Anglican church so he gave him his name, George Bones. So that's how they lost all their names. They lost their original names and took the names of white people. My uncle is 92. He lives in Florida.

Harry: What's his name?

Soleyn: Berisford Sutherland and that's Barat Singh's grandson.

Harry: And those were all farmers, right?

Soleyn: Yes. Well, my mother's father was an entrepreneur. He had three rum shops. He had one here, he had one in Chateaubelair, he had one in Troumaca. So, he had three rum shops. My great grandmother was Huggins from Georgetown, Sarah Huggins. She of course was a homemaker also, she had many children. So, they were not in the labour force out there, they stayed at home.

Harry: So, this is also connected to the Huggins in South Rivers.

Soleyn: Yes, yes, all the Huggins that come from Georgetown. Indian Huggins. I don't know for the other races but I know for the Huggins. The Huggins and I would be related to the Clarkes.

Harry: Your grandparents, where did they reside?

Soleyn: My grandfather on my mother's side lived right here, so I inherited this property (in Rosebank). My grandfather on my father's side lived at Murray's Village, Rocky area in Kingstown.

Harry: Ok.

Soleyn: My grandfather's mother and my grandfather's wife, I didn't know because she died before I came around (was born).

Harry: Alright. What about your relatives, anyone you remember a lot or still stands out, maybe a cousin or somebody who you really got along well with when you were growing up?

Soleyn: Well, the majority of those people would be gone now. They're either dead or migrated but there was the McKenzies, who of course we were related to. This whole Indian community in Rosebank was just one big family where Bharatt Singh left Argyle and came to Rosebank and the rest just followed thinking that there was something of interest in following Bharatt Singh. They ended up here. As close as it seems that the Indians were, there was always rivalry between them as to who will achieve most, you know, who will be the wealthiest one among them. And so, even though you were relatives and you would eat from the same pot, aspiration took a different turn because everybody aspired to be wealthy and in the process of wanting to be wealthy, you didn't care who you kicked down to get to the top. But, if one of them got in trouble with the law, he wouldn't go to jail. They will all band together and bail him out.

Harry: So, it was like this friendly rivalry between them.

Soleyn: Yes, there was always this friendly rivalry between them.

Harry: In terms of your parents and grandparents, did they ever tell you about their fore parents who came from India and their stories about it?

Soleyn: Yeah, but we never really took interest. That's a long-forgotten case. Nobody cared about that, not knowing that somewhere along the line you would have wished that you had listened.

Harry: So, you don't remember any of the names that they mentioned to you, the Indian names?

Soleyn: No, there was never a mention of an Indian name.

Harry: Except for Ram Bharatt Singh?

Soleyn: Yes, they would refer to one another as big popo and little popo, big sister and little sister. And there were certain names that they would call one another, family names, like nicknames but you know for sure that Beharry later became known as McKenzie.

Harry: And that was Beharry from the Richmond estate.

Soleyn: That's right, that's right. And because one was married to the fella from the Richmond estate, she became known as Mrs Richmond. That was my great aunt.

Harry: I see. Is the Richmond surname still around?

Soleyn: No, no, they called her Mrs Richmond but she was married to a Mckenzie. So, the McKenzies are actually descendants of this Beharry fella who was referred to as Mr Richmond.

Harry: You said you didn't know much about them, but in terms of the stories you heard, most of them came on the Richmond estate, right? And worked on this side of the Island. Were those you were connected to?

Soleyn: No, those that I am connected to, came to Rosebank because they had two estates going in Rosebank. One was this estate that stretched from the Bay right up into Rosehall called Linley Valley and there was the other estate which stretched from Chateaubelair (which) goes right up to Top Hill. Top Hill is a 500-acre estate that was owned by Mr McDonald. So, there were two white planters and they were both growing sugar cane because there is an old Works at Petit Bordel, close to the river, going up to the falls and there's an old Works right up at the Anglican church. So, both McDonald and Linley were planting cane but what happened in Rosebank is that after the sugar failed the Indians were able to buy the lands because they were working on the lands. They were working (at) Mr Linley lands. So, Mr Linley said, alright, I am moving out and selling.

Harry: So he went back to England basically.

Soleyn: Yes, he just disappeared, leaving the people, especially the Indians because they were the only ones in a position to buy. And when the Indians actually settled in Rosebank, they were just about five Carib families. So, Rosebank actually belongs to Indians. And when they left Argyle, here is where they settled.

Harry: And then after they sold lands to the different people, different people moved in and intermarried and all of that.

Soleyn: Exactly, but they held onto the farming lands until they died. They were the ones who held onto the farming lands.

Harry: So, today are there a lot of persons of Indian descent living in the Rosebank area?

Soleyn: No, they migrated. There might only be my family. There is Kenard King and there is one Marcella Bacchus. She was an Inspector of Police, named Lester Bacchus' (daughter). He got married to a lady from Georgetown, Crozier. Marcella is his daughter. So, there are just about, maybe five families (remaining).

Harry: Just a small remnant group and it was once predominantly Indians. It was more like what we have with Calder, Argyle where we (had) mostly Indians living in that geographic area?

Soleyn: You see, people were attracted to Rosebank because of the number of pretty Indian girls living in Rosebank.

Harry: Many of them migrated, you said?

Soleyn: Yes, yes, they (are) all gone.

Harry: And they are married overseas to different families. In terms of the earlier times, what are some of the things you remember growing up in this area, this community?

Soleyn: Culturally, there was always the bumdrum. The bumdrum was never a product of the Indian society, it belonged to the Caribs. The Caribs are the ones who are responsible for the bumdrum. The whole thing became intermixed. We see the culture of the Indians fading because even when they had the last one here, I remember, there was an Indian lady up the road, they had brought (an) animal and killed it and they had rice and curry and stuff like that, and they were just eating with their hands. Those are things that we lost. People think it's a disgrace now to eat with your hands. You won't catch even Indians, full blooded Indians now in Rosebank or maybe St. Vincent in general eating with their hands.

Harry: (They use) a knife and fork.

Soleyn: Yes, yes, knife and fork and spoon. But I remember, as a little boy, going to various families. We would go at night and we would play coup and all kinds of ring games and stuff like that. In the day time they would call you, the older Indians, especially the older ladies, and send you to the ends of the earth and you couldn't say no, you weren't going because your mum insisted that you go and if you didn't go, you'd get a licking. And especially those who thought they had money and were wealthier than the average run of the mill, you couldn't say no to them. So, you'd have to go on their lands and pick up coconuts and husk them and bring them home and they would give you a piece of bread. You were well paid, you know. The whole thing is, you couldn't say no. You had to be there. That's one thing they never missed, working you as a slave. Even though they didn't like you and had no interest in you, the only interest was to be able to bring them something beneficial to them. When it comes to your meal and stuff like that, you had to get that for yourself, you know, they wouldn't intercede at that time. But as Indians, we had to go, you know. You had to put in your appearance and be jolly about it. You couldn't sulk. We would go to school, all the Indian children would go to school together, you know. And it seems as though, for some reason, the majority of the Indians excelled in school, better than the other races. Our family in particular, changed the face of education in Rosebank. My mum, from early times, realised that the only way, the only vehicle out of poverty was a good education. She could have been a wealthy woman, but with eleven children to educate and she wanted the best education for them, even though she couldn't afford it. That's why you have all of us, with the exception of me being well educated with a doctorate and Masters. Some of us have more degrees than a thermometer. But I always wanted to make a living from doing business. The thought of working for people never really drove me, I wanted to be my own boss from day one. Well, I went to college in Corpus Christi, Texas but to really sit down and do a doctorate and stuff like that never really appealed to me.

Harry: And how would you say life has changed since then, now compared to then?

Soleyn: Well, life changed, but the driving force behind all the changes, not only in Rosebank but in all of St. Vincent, was the introduction of marijuana. When marijuana came on the scene, everybody became wealthy. Even though you were poor, you thought you were wealthy because you could push your hand in this pocket and pull out five thousand dollars and you push your hand in the next pocket over there and pull out seven thousand dollars. And everybody started to talk to anybody in any old way because now you were no better off than me, I had money just like you. Although a lot of it went up in smoke but that changed the lifestyle especially (in) Rosebank because Rosebank was the early heartland of marijuana.

Harry: Ok, of course, then it was a deeply underground industry unlike now where the dynamics are changing as it relates to the industry.

Soleyn: But then, you could make a thousand for a pound of marijuana. So, I got into it too. I was there. I was planting it. We never smoked it but we sold everything, stem, stick and bush and seed and flowers, everything went. It went (for) between a thousand and eight hundred dollars a pound. So, that's when life changed for everybody.

Harry: And that caused a lot of development.

Soleyn: People wanted to build a bigger house and the competition started. In those days, people never repaired, they replaced.

Harry: So, if you had an old vehicle you bought a new one?

Soleyn: (If you had) a defective vehicle, you get rid of it. You buy another one although it might not have been better than the one that you had. hahaha . Everybody wanted a new one. Everybody wanted a new boat, a new engine. (If) your engine went bad, you pulled the boat up, you took the engine off and you went to Mr Punnett, Pally Punnett. Or you go to this guy Howard and you buy a brand-new engine and put it on your boat because at that time money was flowing in the street. The guys would buy a case of beer, they wouldn't drink half of it. They would mash up most of it on the road and they'd pour it over one another. You had two beers, one in each hand. That's what changed life.

Harry: Tell us about your treasured memories growing up. Some of the things you remembered as a child.

Soleyn: Well, going to the sea on a Sunday until you learn to swim and then when you learn to swim, you could go as often as you want. If you couldn't swim, you had to wait until your parents were going. (If) a big sister or a big brother was going, you would go with them, but once you learn to swim, you were on your own, you could go at any time, go to any beach because you could swim, parents weren't afraid anymore that you would drown. You know, although you could swim, you could still drown.

Going to the lands with my old man (father). We had about fifty acres of land in Windsor Forest. It's only accessible by boat. And so, you would go there with them sometimes on a Saturday. You'll bring home yam and manicou and iguana and stuff like that because the guys used to set manicou pits. (They would) set a can in the ground and bait it up with ripe bananas and of course when you go back (they would catch a lot) because there were tons of manicou in the hills.

You would go rowing, shove down somebody's boat and you go rowing because I mean things were different. The way of life was different, depending on where you lived. In the interior you would go to the river to jam crayfish and things like that. We would be going here on a boat and learning how to fish, you know, learn how to sail a boat, learn how to row a boat.

Harry: You would have had some good times and bad times, some hardships between. (Is there) any of those days you could recall? Things that (were) really challenging.

Soleyn: I remember when we used to drink, mum would go in the back there and get some lemon grass in the morning and she would make your tea with that or (she would) buy some cocoa, chocolate. There was no milk to go with it so you had to drink it just like that. You drink the bush tea just like that and there was yam and maybe potatoes that were boiled and that was all you had. You drink bush tea and yam and you went to school a happy camper. Then I'll drink cocoa, just the cocoa with sugar in it and yam and potatoes as the case might be. At 12 O'clock, there mightn't be anything to eat but you'll get something when you come back in the evening before you go to bed. But I think, what all that did to us was to make us appreciate what we would work for later on in life because you had nothing to start and now you achieve something, only a fool would throw it away. Life was no bed of roses. Life was hard. But we managed. You could think of eleven children (my father) having to look after eleven children and a wife and you didn't have a regular job.

Harry: That must have been a challenge.

Soleyn: You don't know where the next dollar is going to come from. The old man would go and break stones and stuff. Eleven dollars, I think in my time, eleven dollars was for a load of stones (or) there about, you know. That's how he made his living. He (used to) set coal pits because we had a lot of trees on the lands in Windsor Forest. So, he would go up there and set coal pits. But he loved to drink, so most of the time, the money he made, he drank it out, forgetting he had eleven children at home. So life along that line was a real challenge. Back then, you look forward to Christmas where you get a piece of ham and a piece of a loaf of bread. That was good but because of the change in life you could buy a ham every day, you know, you could bake every day. So, those things lost their glitter and improved as people became wealthy but back then a piece of stew pork was a luxury.

Harry: In terms of anything you would want to change, if you had an opportunity to do that during your lifetime, (is there) anything in particular and why would you want to change it?

Soleyn: Well, to tell you the truth, Colvin, if I had to live my life all over again, I'd live it the same way. Maybe without the hardships but if I could change anything in life, it would be to be able to give these young people a good education and teach them about God because this generation now has forgotten God. I would want to give them a good education so at least they won't have to be as ignorant as they are and they won't have to work as hard as they are working now. You know in the age of technology, I guess machinery and computers and stuff like that should be doing the work for you. You do less and more enjoyment of what you work for. Yeah, if I had to change anything, I'd change the way they educate people.

Harry: What about the country as a whole, St. Vincent and the Grenadines, what would you change if you had the power to do so or if you had the capacity to do so?

Soleyn: (The) first thing I'll change is the politicians and hold politicians accountable. Let them declare their assets before they go into politics because like (the calypsonian) Chalkie said before a lot of them get into power they would be able to buy just the coconuts and sell it but (when) they get into (political) power, they buy the estate. You know, after five years they buy the whole estate. So, I would like to see laws set up, integrity legislation, that would say how much money you started with and at the end of your five year or ten-year tenure, how much you ended up with and if there is a discrepancy, jail you. If there is a big discrepancy that you cannot account for then that's poor people's money, you should be jailed.

Harry: In terms of the Foundation itself, the SVG Indian Heritage Foundation, are you aware of the organisation, and if so, what are you aware of in terms of the functions of the organisation?

Soleyn: I am not aware of the full functioning of the organisation because had it not been for Luann and you were there when they came, we would not have been really educated about the heritage and as such the people around here. I think I might know more about the heritage than the others. Even the new members that we recruited. So I think (that) the Heritage (Foundation) has to make a genuine effort to talk to people. Talk to the Indians although there are not many left on this side from Barrouallie down and make them aware of what is going on and how important this is to you as an Indian. What is in it for you? What the Foundation could do for you because you know Colvin everybody wants to know what is in it for me. You know, you just call me up and tell me to join a Foundation, to be part of it. What's in it for either me or my relatives. What is it all about and how could I be a part of it that could be beneficial to me? Not just be a member of the Indian Heritage and that's it, no. A member of the Indian Heritage, oh big deal.

Harry: What about the accomplishments, what would you want to see the organisation do? You have a basic knowledge of what it represents, the people of Indian descent you know making that connection with India, what would you want to see the organisation do?

Soleyn: Well, people want to see something tangible. People want to see that somebody from the village has been elevated to another position and knowing fully well and good that (it) was through the Indian Heritage Foundation. You want to see tangible things happening, things that you could relate to. Then you could say, oh, I am a part of a good organization, a part of an organisation that caters for its people.

Harry: Alright, I think, that's about it. Did you enjoy sharing the story and chatting and reflections?

Soleyn: Oh, yeah. It's always good to chat with, as the fella says, it's always good to chat with family. Haha.

Harry: Thanks very much for taking the time out to talk to me about this.

Commentary on interview with Mr Noel Soleyn

The story of the Indians in Rosebank as narrated by Mr Soleyn is similar to that of the other villages where the Indians settled after the plantation system was abandoned. The Indians took the western names of their godfathers and their children were christened with new names. Their culture gradually faded. The habit of eating with hands disappeared and the methods of cooking became more westernised. Their appreciation of Indian music became dimmer as they began adopting the local Carib drumming and other forms of Creole and American music. Most Indian families, like those in other parts of St. Vincent, migrated, to the extent for example, that only about about five Indian families now remain in Rosebank. However, there are also some unique aspects of the village of Rosebank.

Choosing a Village to Settle

After indentureship, although the Indians were scattered throughout St. Vincent, most of them settled in a few villages and a town that appeared to have been consciously or subconsciously selected based on factors related to ensuring their survival and which offered better opportunities. These villages include Park Hill, Argyle, Yambou, Calder, Akers, Richland Park, Rosehall plus Georgetown. The main criteria in settling in these areas appeared to be a good source of water, either a river or spring and available lands for agriculture and housing.

One Indian from an Indian delegation who visited Montreal, Richland Park recently remarked that the ex-indentured Indians could have chosen Richland Park because it may have reminded them of the villages they came from in India. Although some of their generations who came from Argyle to Richland Park may not have seen or remembered the villages in India as they arrived as children (Thomas Seetaram Woods and James Pa Thomas for example) and were very young, they would have heard the stories of their elders.

According to Mr Soleyn, Indian men also moved from Argyle to Rosebank as they were attracted by the beautiful women living there. Argyle was also known as a place where Indians on the Windward side of the Island visited to find part-ners. Some of the families in Georgetown consist of ancestors who first resided at Argyle. It appeared that men found it a bit difficult to find a partner locally in some cases. This is supported by the fact that the register of the Indians who came to St. Vincent has a ratio of only about or less than one woman to two men and also because at the time, Indian men did not generally marry outside of their race. One estate overseer is even reported to have said that one woman was adequate for two men.

Mr Soleyn also said that many Indians came from Argyle to Rosebank follow-ing Mr Bharatt Singh's lead. Interestingly, Mr Soleyn said that Mr Singh came to St. Vincent in 1862 but I wasn't able to find Mr Singh's name in the ship's record of 1862, neither on any of the other ships. Did he migrate from another Island? These reports need further investigation. What is clear is that at that time the operations of the estates at Rosebank had become unprofitable and the white planters wanted to sell out and move back to England. The price of land was therefore relatively cheap and this was an attraction for the Indians. The Indians had some savings and according to Mr Soleyn, they were the only ones in a position to buy lands. His father later owned 50 acres at Windsor Forest, North of Rosebank. It is remarkable that the whole of Rosebank at one time, as Mr Soyleyn indicated, was owned almost totally by only Indians.

The news may therefore have spread that not only were there pretty girls in Rosebank but that agricultural land was available. In addition, there was the possibility for fishing as Rosebank has a calm bay, being on the western side of the Island. Fishing later became one of the activities of the residents of Rosebank. Fish from seine fishing on this side of the Island were known to be distributed in later years to villages as far as Richland Park. Mr Glaston Woods, Mr Philbert Thomas and Mr Lloyd Bacchus are known to have conducted this trade.

Friendly Rivalry among the Indians

Mr Soleyn referred to a rivalry that existed among the Indians in Rosebank where they would strive to become the wealthiest even at the expense of other Indians. Whereas this situation may have existed in Rosebank, I haven't seen evidence in other parts of St. Vincent where Indians will "kick down" other Indians to get to the top. He further stated however that if one Indian got in trouble with the law, the others would nevertheless rally around to help and support him.

The Indians in St. Vincent aspired to improve their economic situations and worked towards that, by getting into businesses. Whereas one of Mr Soleyn's relatives had three "rum shops" in Rosebank, most of the Indians in St. Vincent who ran shops, operated grocery shops, some of which also sold alcohol. This was the case in other villages such as Calder and Georgetown. In Richland Park, none of the shops operated by Indians sold alcohol as they became predominantly Seventh Day Adventists.

Yes, the Indians were aspirational and ambitious. This was evident not only in business ventures but in educational pursuits. Many Indians excelled and went abroad to further their education. Notwithstanding the limited opportunities in St. Vincent, as Mr Soleyn admitted, the Indian children in Rosebank excelled and did comparatively better than others.

Marijuana

Mr Soleyn outlined a change in the economic situation of the villagers in Rosebank that was due to the production and sale of marijuana. This phenomenon was fairly recent in the 1980s onwards by which time most of the Indians in St. Vincent had migrated so only a few of the Indians may have been involved when compared to the wider population in Rosebank.

Marijuana was used prior to the 1950s by some of the Indians in St. Vincent. At that time, it was referred to as Ganga. This plant may have been brought from India by the Indians during the time of indentureship as were other plants such as mangoes and susumba. I was told that some of my ancestors in Richland Park used to smoke the ganga in big pipes (Chillum). At that time, it was not illegal to do so.

CHAPTER 10

Interview with Mr Winston Bacchus

Bacchus: I am Winston Bacchus of Richland Park, retired Education Officer. My family came out of the belly of indentured labourers from India on the Argyle estate. My grandmother came from India as a young girl. She married Ridley Bacchus, also of Argyle and produced a large family. My father Nathaniel, their first son, married Beatrice Sutherland, also born on the Argyle estate and the marriage produced 12 children. When the estate changed hands, they moved to Richland Park and built a small, wooden house with an outdoor toilet and a detached kitchen. They were very poor and they eked out a living doing agriculture on a small bit of land they had bought. They had twelve children, four boys, Gerald, Lauren, Grafton and Winston and eight girls, Vernie, Claurice, Elrita, Albertina, Ida, Inez, Ermine and Evelyn. Only two boys and three girls remain. My father Nathaniel Bacchus died in 1988 at the age of 96 years and my mother died in 1960 at the age of 60 years.

On a personal note, I attended the Marriaqua Government all age primary school where I sat the internal primary school education exam. I did very well. As a result, I was selected as a pupil teacher and posted to the Evesham Methodist School at the age of 15 years. The colonial system of education was such that you learn to teach by trial and error. As a grade one pupil teacher, I attended the Pupil Teacher's Training Centre, first in Kingstown at the then, Richmond Hill Government School and later at the Stubbs Pupil Teacher's Training Centre two days per week for academic training. I passed the annual exams from grade one to grade two, from grade two to grade three and was promoted to a student teacher grade to prepare for the external Senior Cambridge Exam which I sat and passed in seven subjects. As a result, I was promoted to a Probationary Assistant Teacher Grade for two years and then to be certificated as Assistant Teacher Grade after one year.

I taught in several schools at all levels from kindergarten to seniors at Marriaqua Government, Richland Park Government, Belair Government, Belmont Government and Evesham Methodist School. There was no Teachers' College in St. Vincent but the government sent one or two senior teachers to the Erdiston Teachers College in Barbados for two years. There was a great need for teacher training and in 1964 the government opened the St. Vincent Teachers Training

College which was housed in the old wooden Grammar School building. I was among the first intake of thirty teachers. The principal was a retired Canadian teacher, Mr E. W. Holmes. I graduated with honours and was appointed head-teacher of the Evesham Methodist School.

Then, I was appointed head of the Stubbs Teachers Training Centre where we prepared teachers for the external Senior Cambridge Exam. Then I moved to the Biabou Methodist School as Headteacher and later to the Wesley Hall Methodist School in Kingstown which is no more and was converted to the C. W. Prescott School at Richmond Hill.

In 1968, I was awarded a Commonwealth Scholarship to the University of the West Indies at the Mona Campus in Jamaica where I completed my degree in Education. On my return from UWI, I was appointed Education Officer with responsibility for supervision of all primary schools in St. Vincent, from Fancy to Union Island. When I visited the Grenadines, I had to travel by a boat called Friendship Rose. It was really scary, especially when crossing the Bequia Channel. Anyhow, I survived, thanks to God.

In 1970, Sir Rupert John was appointed Governor of St. Vincent. He was the first native to hold that position. Sir Rupert, who hailed from Evesham, village was a well-educated man and was very interested in the education of the children of SVG. He told the Chief Education Officer that he wanted to visit as many of the primary schools as possible and I as Education Officer was designated to accompany Sir Rupert on these school visits. We arrived at the schools around prayer time and assembly time. After prayers, Sir Rupert would address the entire school for about half an hour. After a few visits, Sir Rupert suggested that he would like to see the children repeat a pledge of loyalty to St. Vincent each morning after prayers. He asked me to make up a suitable pledge. So, on our next visit, I showed him the pledge which I made up and he agreed that it was appropriate.

This is the school pledge. *Land of my birth, I pledge to thee my loyalty and devotion in all I think or speak or do.* The Ministry of Education, having given its approval, sent the pledge in a circular to all primary schools asking teachers to get the students to memorise it and to recite it each morning after prayers. That's how the school pledge was born, created by Education Officer, Winston Bacchus.

After a time, there was a shortage of lecturers at the Teachers Training College and I was seconded for one academic year as lecturer in Principles of Teaching, Psychology of Teaching and the Teaching of English. Then, I reverted to my substantive position as Education Officer.

When I retired from the service, I had taught in all sections of the primary schools during my twenty years as a teacher and twenty years in administration as Education Officer. As part of my civic duties, I had to conduct General Elections in Marriaqua Constituency as a Returning Officer on several occasions. I was appointed a Justice of the Peace and assisted many persons in the preparation of legal documents like applications for passports and birth certificates, preparation of Wills et cetera. In recognition of my services in Education, I was awarded the MBE, Member of the British Empire, by the Queen and I went to Buckingham Palace for the installation in 2011.

In 1958, I married Perlina Gibson of Fountain and had five children, Wendy, Evande, Karen, Colin and Andre. This is a synopsis of my life, prepared for the Indian Heritage Foundation 2020, but there are many other activities not mentioned, in which I was engaged. Winston Bacchus, Richland Park, Retired Education Officer.

Harry: Wow! Ok, you pretty much answered most of the questions I had here. The other thing I had to ask you was about your grandparents, you didn't mention your grandparents and those you grew up with.

Bacchus: Well, my grandparents...

Harry: (Do) you know much about them?

Bacchus: Not very much. As I mentioned, I understand my grandmother came from India as a young girl (Bhugmonti) but I don't have any information about her background. My grandfather was Ridley Bacchus, I don't know if he was born on an estate in Argyle or (if) he came from India. I don't have that information but they got married in Argyle.

Harry: You said you don't remember any of those Indian names, they didn't mention any other than your grandfather, (did they)?

Bacchus: No, I can't recall their Indian names.

Harry: What about when you were growing up as a youngster, some of the things you remember about your way of life back then.

Bacchus: Well, my parents lived by agriculture and as children, we were labourers on the bit of land. They never hired anybody to work because they had so many (children), it's twelve children they had. And we had to do agricultural (work). We had to mind the goat, the donkey, the cattle and all the animals. Then we had to run off to school down Mespo from Richland Park on a stony road. That is the kind of life we had. And sometimes you're sick because a lot of diseases were prevalent, yaws and tobo, jigger and so on and I had my share of it. That is the kind of life I had.

Harry: So, most of the family was agriculture based. It was the land.

Bacchus: And all my brothers and sisters only had primary school education. You see, I am the only one out of the lot. No, one other sister who is in England had a secondary education and teaching but they all worked on the lands until they became older, they married and they moved out and so forth and so on.

Harry: Ok. (Can you) remind me of your age before we go further?

Bacchus: 85

Harry: 85. Ok. What would you say is different now when you look at life, compared to back then?

Bacchus: Well, life in those days was very much more social, that is, you were able to move in and out of your family, you know, you played together, you ate together and everybody loved one another. You never had these kinds of things that's going on these days. Now, everybody is in their house, you can hardly see them. You see so many burglar bars around the houses, so everybody is more confined now and selfish than in those days because you would have a mango and you take a bite and you give your other friend a bite and another one a bite and that sort of thing, you know. You see, so I would say that life in those days was much happier than nowadays.

Harry: In terms of when you were growing up, am sure you would have had some cherished memories, somethings you remember most as a child, do you have anything you wish to add?

Bacchus: Well, as I said, we were more agricultural-based and every August, my father would kill a goat and we would have Portuguese yam and mutton, a big pot of mutton and a big pot of Portuguese yam and breadfruit and dasheen and so on. Those were happy memories. At Christmas time, we all celebrated Christmas. We didn't have much but you would get a little whistle, the girls would get a little Christmas basket and so forth and you think that was great. You see, in our time, those were happy moments, especially, as children in a home, we played together, we had our nice time together, you know. We would go out in the moonlight and play coop around the village with our cousins and so on, you know. Everybody lived so nice and happy together. But Christmas and August, August is Emancipation Day. They remember Emancipation Day, you see, and my parents used to have something special for the family on Emancipation Day.

Harry: Well, in all of that, yes, you had good memories but there may have been some hardships and some difficult times that you faced, (are there) any of those you can recall?

Bacchus: Yes, yes, diseases were very prevalent and that's one of the things I suffered from because it kept me from school, sometimes for a whole month. You're barefoot, your parents can't buy a soft-mash, (and) give it to you, you have to walk on the gravel stone. Whether you like it or not, they send you to school. You see. And I suffered from diseases. I had yaws, I had tobo, I had jiggers and all of that but still I didn't make those things keep me from learning and I went to school and I don't boast but I was a bright student. The teacher skipped me in some classes and I reached up to Standard 6. In those days it was Standard 1 to Standard 6. We had the Infants and the Kindergarten and then we had (classes) from Standard 1 to Standard 6 and even to Standard 7. And you leave school at 15 years old. That was the school leaving age. And if it is possible that you could find some little things to do , you do it because unemployment was rampant and the only avenue was either a civil servant or a policeman, those are the only things. And (for a) civil servant, everybody had to go to Kingstown. If you don't have transportation, you have to take the bus. And I didn't like to be a policeman and I didn't have the wherewithal to go to town, so I was so happy when they chose me to teach. You see, I made a lot of progress in my teaching career and there it is.

Harry: If you were to change anything about your life, what would that be?

Bacchus: That's a difficult question but I think in my years when I suffered from diseases, I would've loved to see that change. And when I became an Education Officer, I had a lot of racial slurs against me because I was the only Indian person to ever become an education officer. There were Indian headteachers, but I was and I am the only one so far to become an Education officer. And many of the teachers turned their backs against me when I visited. I had to visit all the schools. You know, as an Education Officer, you have your schools. Every school you had to visit and see how things are going, whether the teachers are doing right and so forth and so on. And some of them you hear make the slur, this coolie man, you know, that is one of the things that I didn't like. But I didn't (care), you know, I just shrugged my shoulders off it and after a while, they stopped. But this racial thing is there, even up to today in St. Vincent. And to get promotion, they look at race too.

I would like to tell you something. When I was awarded the scholarship to go to UWI and the Chief Personnel Officer didn't know who I was, they thought I was a negro and when I was supposed to reach university on the first of October I didn't get there until a week after because the Permanent Secretary in the Ministry of Social Affairs, it was Social Affairs and Education joined together, had my file on his desk and would not pay attention to it. And the professor from the university had to call St. Vincent and say where is Winston Bacchus? He is supposed to have been here at the university since the first of October. And I had to rush to get there by the fourth of October, the next week. So, you know, that thing is there. It mightn't expose itself so blatantly nowadays but it is there underneath.

Harry: In terms of the country as a whole, (is there) anything that you would have changed if you had the opportunity to have any level of influence on making changes in the country?

Bacchus: I think people are too divided in St. Vincent, they're politically divided and the politics has infiltrated even in the home among families. There are families now who are divided because of their political affiliation. And it has even reached churches. So that's one of the things that I would really like to see (changed). I don't know if there is another system that we can devise that would bring people together. But that division of people in St. Vincent, and it is not only in St. Vincent, I must say, it happens throughout many countries even in the United States (of America) you have it. But people have to live more lovingly and be kind to each other. That's one of the things I would like to see. And the country is making progress, you know, but it is sort of lopsided because one set of people feel they are not contributing to anything. Only one set of people (who are) contributing to it. So, there is a need for togetherness.

Harry: In terms of the Foundation itself, the SVG Indian Heritage Foundation, what do you know about the organisation?

Bacchus: Well, I read about it and I listened to them but I am not physically well these days. I have a number of health issues and I have to walk with a cane. I can't walk out again to go anywhere. Am more confined, you see, but I usually look at the programs they have and keep in touch with the newspapers but to be present at the functions, I can't make it.

Harry: What would you like to see the Foundation accomplished in its day to day tasks?

Bacchus: Well, if India can help a little more, maybe to set up a school or some learning Institution in St. Vincent. Well India is helping St. Vincent but you know these bilateral arrangements, when they give you some money, they put conditions on it. You can't use it for certain purposes and India itself has so many poor people, you know, and if they can help St. Vincent and help the Indian Heritage Foundation to maybe set up some school or something of the sort, that might be a good idea.

Harry: Ok, so I believe that is all, (is there) anything else you would like to add?

Bacchus: No, I think I have given you quite a bit and as I said, this is only a synopsis of what I have done because there are lots of other things, (such as) civic duties that I have performed. I have a connection with churches. I am a local preacher in our church, the Methodist Church and I do a lot of religious work. I used to teach Sunday School and all those things in church organisations but I can't do them again because I am more or less handicap now, you see.

Harry: Did you enjoy sharing the story and talking to us today?

Bacchus: Yes, I wanted to see you especially.

Commentary on interview with Mr Winston Bacchus

Mr Winston Bacchus gave a succinct synopsis of the story of the Indians coming "out of the belly of indentureship," their new birth and growth. Two of his great grandfather Rambaluck Singh's seven sons and one of Rambaluck Singh's two daughters left the Argyle estate and moved to Richland Park. All of them and their children had many children averaging about 10 each. One of Mr Winston Bacchus' paternal uncles, Mr Norman Bacchus, had fifteen children with his first wife Mrs Muriel Bacchus. Mr Norman Bacchus depended on the operation of a grocery shop and like most of the other villagers he also managed a farm to support his huge family. Life was hard for some but over the years their economic situation improved as some got involved in light manufacturing, small businesses and more commercial farming operations especially during the 1960s to 80s when bananas were green gold. A few like Mr Winston Bacchus had the opportunity to enter the teaching profession, but in subsequent generations several more became teachers. One important development that contributed to this was the establishment of the SDA primary and secondary schools in the village.

Indians in the teaching profession

In several villages in St. Vincent there were hardly any teachers of Indian descent prior to the 1950s but as the education system developed and with the establishment of the St. Vincent Teachers Training College in 1964 several more Indians got the opportunity to become teachers. In my family for example, most of the children were expected to become teachers and five of the 10 siblings were at one time teachers, one Mr Hugh Thomas was a headteacher and one Mrs Anita Thomas, a university lecturer. So, from the 1960s onwards more Indians like the other ethnic groups in St. Vincent entered the teaching profession while some also entered the Civil Service.

It is exceptional and remarkable that Mr Winston Bacchus was selected in the early years to be trained as a professional teacher. It is even more remarkable that he was appointed to work as an Education Officer, a position which no other Indian has been given since. St. Vincent and the Grenadines will remember him for the national school pledge he created. *Land of my birth, I pledge to thee my loyalty and devotion in all I think or speak or do.* We congratulate him for being awarded the MBE by the Queen of Britain and the Commonwealth, an award that only a few persons of Indian heritage obtained.

Racism in the workplace and in awarding of scholarships

Mr Winston Bacchus said he had to endure blatant racist slurs and negative attitudes of some teachers who even turned their backs towards him, when he visited the schools. This is a demonstration of the racism that existed over the years towards Indians by some people of other races. Racism in the workplace by people in professional occupations in schools operated by the government is absolutely unacceptable. There has been and there will most likely continue to be some forms of racism in society among different races but it can be particularly damaging when it takes place in the workplace.

The fact that the Chief Personnel Officer colluded with the Permanent Secretary in the Ministry of Social Affairs to stall the processing of his scholarship when they discovered that Mr Winston Bacchus was an Indian speaks volumes to the racism that existed in the public service and government institutions. The Permanent Secretary had Mr Bacchus' file on his desk and would not pay attention to it, nor did the Chief Personnel Officer follow this up. There are other cases that I know of when similar things happened to prevent Indians from getting promotions, appointments and scholarships. This could have contributed to the wave of migration among the Indians during the 1960s to the 1980s.

It is notable that there were some changes when the Mitchel government took the reins of the country from 1984 and later the Gonsalves government in 2002. However, although these governments generally do not condone racism, there are still people in some critical positions who would treat Indians unfairly under various other guises.

Mr Bacchus regrets the political divisions within the country that have infiltrated and affected relationships within homes and churches. The Indians in general in St. Vincent and the Grenadines have never sided with one political party or the other as is the case in Trinidad and Guyana. There seems to be equal support of either party by the Indians and vice versa. This was aptly demonstrated when both parties unanimously approved an Act to recognise June 1 as Indian Arrival Day and October 7th as Indian Heritage Day on March 26th, 2007.

Outstanding Vincentians of Indian Heritage

Other than Mr Winston Bacchus there are other Vincentians of Indian heritage who have made outstanding and stalwart contributions to St. Vincent and the Grenadines and in the diaspora. These include:

Dr Gideon Cordice - Public Health

Mr Lester Bacchus - Police Service

Mr Teroy Bacchus - Insurance Services

Mr Donelly Bacchus - Farming - Kelly Par Boxing Plant

Dr St. Clair Thomas - Chief Medical Officer

Mr Evans Morgan - Politician and Educator

Mr Cenio Lewis - High Commissioner, UK

Dr Gideon Lewis - Medical Services, USA

Drs Kamal and Rafeek Woods- Medical Services, USA

Mr Nathaniel Jack - Manufacturing and Retail plus Queens Award

Mr Vincent Thomas - Wholesale distribution

Mr Das Dasilva and son Kenneth - Manufacturing and distribution

Mrs Judith Jones Morgan - Attorney General and CMG Award

Mr Norris Deane - Pharmacist and Vice president of the Lions Club SVG

Dr Raphael Lewis - Dentist

Mr Norris Bullock - Mayor in Luton, UK

Dr Denzil Soleyn - Teacher

Mr Lennox Bowman - CEO of GECCU et al

Mr Herman Fraser Young - Politician

Mr Henrick Bullock -Passenger transport and Trucking

Mr Arnot Paynter - Dentist

Mr Randolph Toussaint - Police Commissioner

Mr Randolph Russel - Politician and businessman

Mr Daniel Gaymes - Pharmacist

Mr Edison Bowman - Pharmacist

Mr Horace Crichton - Pharmacist

Mr Ronnie Marks - Lawyer

Mr Alrick Hillocks - Businessman

Mr Denzil Bacchus - Jewelry manufacturer and retail

Mrs Cheryl Dean Rodriguez - Beauty Shows producer and Banker

Dr Lawson Moore - Dentist

Dr Grantley Joseph - Medical Services

Pastor Dermoth Baptiste - President of the SDA Mission in SVG

Mr Ormon and Aliena Baptiste - Manufacturing and retail

Chapter 11

Interview with Mrs Sadie Bowman

Harry: (Can you) tell me your full name and your occupation please?

Bowman: Sadie Ann Myrtle Bowman.

Harry: And where do you currently live?

Bowman: This is Richland Park and it's here I (was) born and (grew up). (Do) you understand? Yeah.

Harry: Your parents name and what they did, (do) you remember any of those?

Bowman: My parents (were) Enid and Henry Bacchus.

Harry: And what did they do for a living?

Bowman: Well, just (running the) plantation and taking care of animals.

Harry: So, they were farmers.

Bowman: Yes, so to speak.

Harry: Your brothers and your sisters' names, (do) you recall those?

Bowman: Wilmoth Bacchus and Eucina. Well, she (is) married to a Mounsey but at least before (she was) a Bacchus. We were Bacchus before we got married.

Harry: What about your children?

Bowman: Ok. Kethlene, Yvette, Kemston, Linessa, Amy, Ena, Ruth, Samuel.

Harry: They are based overseas, they are not in St. Vincent, (right)?

Bowman: Three of them, three girls are here because I was asking the same lady who did point you on to us, she said she knows Ena very much, both of them are good friends.

Harry: Ok. Do you know any of your uncles and your aunts and their names?

Bowman: My uncle and aunts on my mother's side, ok. (We) got Cephus, Albion, Austin, Levi, Estelle, Rita, Sheila, Enid, that's my mother. Those are my aunties and uncles.

Harry: And what about your grandparents, do you know anything about your grandparents whether on your dad or mum's side?

Bowman: My grandparents on my father's side, well, "long time" (ago) people didn't used to communicate with one another so…

Harry: So, you don't know much about them?

Bowman: No, no.

Harry: But do you know if they were from Richland Park?

Bowman: Yes, I think my grandmother was from Richland Park and my father. (In those) days, they called him Jeet, Jeet Bacchus and (my grandmother) name was Caroline.

Harry: And what about your other relatives? Did you have any relatives growing up that you were close to? I don't know if you had cousins or other people in the family that you were close to.

Bowman: You know, the family just scattered away and sometimes you don't have the communication and to chat with one another and to know how it's running.

Harry: You don't know a lot of your relatives, a lot of connections with them.

Bowman: Well the uncles and the aunties were usually together, like the names that I just called but (those) like the older heads on my mother's side, I don't really know them. You know what I mean, just the aunties and the uncles.

Harry: (Did) they ever tell you about your connection with India, like those who came before? Any of the names, any Indian names?

Bowman: No, as I said, the older heads didn't sit down and discuss our relatives from India. Well, those who came from India like our grandparents, and that is it. Otherwise, we didn't have any communication with the former set of people.

Harry. Ok. So as it relates to the way they lived, all you know is that some were from Calder. One side of the family from Calder and the other side from Richland Park?

Bowman: Right, and some from Park Hill because daddy (my husband) and the others you know.

Harry: What about the family from Park Hill, those people in Park Hill?

Bowman: Castello and Latchman. Lots of Bacchus live here. On my daddy side, you have a lot of Bacchus living here.

Harry: In terms of what you remember growing up, the younger days growing up and what life was like for you.

Bowman: Well, I can tell you I went to school and I (got) sick and I couldn't really concentrate as I should and taking care of the animals and so on. Sometimes when it's raining, you get your clothes wet and you don't think about anything about that and my hair was long and thick and then I caught a bad cold. I caught a bad cold, my brother. And from then, I couldn't even go to school and I reached Class 3, just Class 3. At least, you know, I tried to read on my own after my sickness went away. But otherwise, I didn't go along but after I married we were in farming. Well, he had two cattle and whatever but he (got) sick too. And the children that come up now, we try to educate them. And everybody has a little education and they are able to do some little things for themselves.

Harry: Would you say, life is different now than back then, how is it different?

Bowman: It's different because people now, after you educate yourself, right, you (are) able to get a little more money. You can see life differently because in (the olden) days, you don't have anything. You might kill a pig or a goat and you know, and try to eat from that and whatsoever but things now (are) better. When you look around, you don't have to, like our children now, they don't have to go so much now to the garden and do anything. And their husbands might plant a little dasheen and whatever but not as we used to work hard because as I said, we used to take care of the animals and the little gardening and that's it. But people can work now, they educate themselves. They see life differently and they can, when the month comes, give you a little penny. Not my children alone you know but other children in the community.

Harry: When you were growing up, there might have been things that you remember more, some treasured memories, some things that you can always remember, good times, (are there) any of those that come to mind?

Bowman: Well, you know, in the olden days, children were not as rude as now. We used go into one another's yard and used to skip together or have a little round dodge together. And then, in the evening when you got home you had to go and tote water because we didn't have any pipe (water) like people have now. We are used to having pipe (water) now but in our days, we had to go (to fetch water). Well, we had a place out there, we called it spring, Sterling Spring, so we used to go there and fetch water and get back home, wash the dishes and cook and so on. And (for) washing of the clothes, we had to go to the river. So, it was harder than now because I mean you have to work to pay your bills but remember you have every convenience (at) home. You have your little washing machine, you have water to cook, you know what I mean and so on.

Harry: But (is there) anything that stands out, in terms of hard times that you experienced, things that you really remember, tough things that you went through?

Bowman: My parents used to work very hard and we used to have to go to tote the manure. When I say manure, the animal's manure, you know what I mean.

Harry: Animal dung, yeah.

Bowman: Yeah, then we too, well myself had to leave home and go to the mountain and take lunch, breakfast to the people who were working with us. And I used to go and help pack the bananas in the boxes. And sometimes we planted (a) little yam and so on and we used to plant, what you call it, Portuguese yams. And we used to get them and ship them. When I say ship them, (I mean) take them to the market like Young Island. I used to go there and sell 400 pounds or 500 (pounds). Yeah, we just get them and take them there. A bus would take me from the junction (in Richland Park) and take me right down to the road that goes over to Young Island. So, we managed after a while, you know. As you go along life's journey, you see things look different but it was very hard. But never mind, God is in control and He knows what is best for His children. So, God sees me through. He sees us through.

Harry: Alright, if you had a chance to change anything in your life growing up, and you're looking back at it now, what would you change?

Bowman: Well, if I really wasn't sick, things would have been different but I was really sick, you know.

Harry: So you wish you weren't sick at that time, so you could (have) finished school?

Bowman: Yeah, yeah, (at) nine years I had to stop school but thank God still I could read and write a little. I could communicate with somebody and the children as they grow up, I taught them the way of leading them to God. You understand?

Harry: Ok, great

Bowman: And that is very good for me, individually, because what can I do? Having the children, just leave them alone? No, no, God told me that I must take care of them physically and spiritually. I worked very hard. Never mind, God saw me through.

Harry: If you had an opportunity, a chance to change certain things in St. Vincent and the Grenadines what would that be? (Is there) anything about the country (that) you would change and why?

Bowman: You know brother, I don't think about all those things. Long time ago, all you knew was that your parents were poor, and you try to cooperate with them until you take responsibility and you see life differently because having children, then you have to work hard for them. You understand, to send them to school because well we sent them to government school but before that we used to send them to...

Harry: Private school?

Bowman: Yeah, the Adventist schools, primary and then the secondary school.

Harry: Mountain View?

Bowman: Right, right and from there, they got big and they got a little teaching job, not all of them, (but) they're good, they're good.

Harry: Do you know about the Indian Heritage Foundation and if so what do you know about the organisation?

Bowman: All I know (is) that some of the Indians came from India and they come and spread out themselves here and there and everywhere.

Harry: The organisation exists to highlight, you know, the Indian presence in St. Vincent and the Grenadines. So, what we are trying to do is to make the connection with India and basically look to the motherland for the connections so that our people can know where they came from and know all the family connections, who they are related to and the struggles of the Indians who came here as well and the life that they lived. So, that is why we are here and that is why we are documenting what you have to say and others have to say about growing up as an Indian in your community.

Bowman: Oh, oh. Ok, ok.

Harry: So, that is what the organisation is about.

Bowman. So, when you take all these statements from whosoever, what are you going to do now?

Harry: We are doing individual presentations that persons all over the World can listen to, (those) who follow the organization and anybody who wants to hear about the story about the Indians. So, we'll make it available so that they can hear the story and how everybody grew up and what things were like in their days.

Bowman: Who are you speaking to now from India?

Harry: We have a connection with the Ambassador in Suriname and he is in contact with India. So we have to go through the Ambassador and the Ambassador will talk to India on our behalf to the government of India but we have a connection with India.

Bowman: So, what are they going to do now? Even though they have connections with India, what are they going to do with these people, the younger heads?

Harry: Well, we're building the relationship with them so that we can get opportunities, maybe even scholarships, people can go to India and see what India is like, get to study in India and we get India to help us with certain things here, maybe in education in different areas. So, that's why we're building that relationship.

Bowman: Ok

Harry: What would you like to see the organisation do, the Indian Heritage Foundation, to better represent the local population in St. Vincent?

Bowman: This is all the answer I can make to you but for me, connections with other people and whatsoever, right now I don't go anywhere and there's hardly any Indians now who you can go to and talk with one another, you understand.

Harry: So, you want us to be able to talk to more of the old people, the older people and find out from them about the Indian lifestyle. Those that remember?

Bowman: Yes, yes.

Harry: So, (did) you enjoy the little talk and the exchange we had?

Bowman: Oh yes, oh yes, oh yes.

Harry: Alright, so, let me thank you very much and wish you all the best.

Commentary on İnterview with Mrs Sadie Ann Bowman

The genealogy of the Indians in Richland Park

The story presented by Mrs Sadie Ann Bowman painted a typical scenario of an Indian village. A few family members would have come from the estates after indentureship and they would have had large numbers of children, as would the next two or three generations. She pointed out that there were a lot of Bacchuses in that village. The Indians in this area were also related to those in Calder, Park Hill and other villages. Some of the well-known Indian family names in Richland Park were the Bacchus, Thomas, Woods, Moore, Joseph, Lewis, Bowman, Morgan, McDowall and Williams.

The ancestors of these families in Richland Park were either born on other estates or came to St. Vincent as children. For example, the Bacchus family in Richland Park was started by the two sons of Rambaluck Singh, Ridley "Babu" Bacchus and "Hanuman" Bacchus who were born on the Argyle estate. The Thomas family were descendants of James Thomas from Lot 14 estate beyond the Rabacca Dry river, who came as a child to St. Vincent. The Woods family were descendants of Thomas "Seetaram" Woods from Argyle who also came as a child at the age of three years with his father Kowlessur and mother Bachia. The Moore family and the maternal ancestor of the Joseph family were children of John Ahkoo from the Argyle estate. There were intermarriages in the next generations and all of these families became blood relatives.

The evolution of Agriculture in Indian Villages

As in most of the other villages in St. Vincent and the Grenadines people depended heavily on agriculture. After indentureship sugar cane was replaced by cotton and arrowroot and in the 1950s bananas. Root crops such as yams, cassava, sweet potatoes, peanuts, dasheen, tannia, eddoes and other vegetables and fruits were always planted for local consumption. Some of the root crops, dasheen, eddoes and small animals were also exported mainly during the period 1960 to 1990. Coconuts, cocoa and corn were also grown to produce cooking oil, chocolate sticks and corn meal. However, sugar cane, cotton, arrowroot and bananas were the main crops grown for export.

Some of the Indians who purchased lands after indentureship also tried their hand at growing sugar cane, cotton and arrowroot to supply the factories operated by the government but these businesses didn't last as they were not viable at the time. In the 1960s,, 70s and 80s several Indians were involved with the commercial production of bananas which was profitable for a long period of time and from which a weekly income could be earned throughout the year.

With the WTO rulings on the trade of bananas and the removal of preferential treatment from the Windward Islands for the import of bananas into the UK the banana industry collapsed. Whereas agriculture contributed over 60% of GDP when the banana crop was king in St. Vincent, its contribution was by 2020 less than 11%. During the last quarter of the twentieth century also many of the Indians in St. Vincent migrated to England and North America as there were better economic and educational opportunities available. Like others in the general population, most of the remaining Indians in St. Vincent have moved out of commercial agriculture to having only kitchen gardens.

Changes in Indian Village Life - 4th and 5th generations

Mrs Sadie Ann Bowman still plants her kitchen garden, as do some of her children. However, although she only received a limited education reaching Standard 3, it is important to note that she ensured that her children got a better education. Secondary education was made available by the Mountain View Adventist Academy (MVAA) and some of her children were able to go on to further education in teaching and other professions. Whereas most Indians were dependent on agriculture, they are now involved in office work or teaching. With a more reliable income from these jobs, they were able to build better houses. When the Indians moved off the estates, some lived in wattle and daub houses. When Riley "Babu" Bacchus moved to Richland Park, he could only afford a small wooden house with an outdoor toilet and a detached kitchen. The third generation were later able to build modest concrete structures with all the necessary facilities. This development was the trend for all the people in St. Vincent as the government was able to improve the infrastructure of the villages. Better pitched and concrete roads, retaining walls and bridges were built. Pipe borne water was made available as well as electricity and later the telephone.

The 4th and 5th generations built more luxurious houses as their economic situation improved and also because some who had migrated returned home with their savings. Sadly, some of the fun of carrying water from the springs or playing round dodge and other games, as Mrs Sadie Ann Bowman pointed out, have virtually disappeared and gave way to other activities such as watching television and looking at mobile phones.

Interviewees Views about The SVG Indian Heritage Foundation

All participants of these interviews were asked if they knew about the Foundation and what they would like to see it do. All of them knew of the organisation and some participated in a few of its activities. Mrs Theresa Jack said that she would like to see the people of Indian descent interact more as it was in her younger days and re-establish closer relationships and values of love for each other. Mrs Sadie Ann Bowman reminisces about the time when she was a child, when children would visit each other's home and skip and play round dodge games. Mr Patrick Deane also remembers the times when children used to play cricket with young breadfruit and orange balls and Mr Winston Bacchus remembers the days and nights when he could play games in the village with his cousins. These are some of the relationships and values that the interviewees would like to see come back to life.

Mr Soleyn indicated that people should not merely be members of an organisation but that the organisation, such as the SVG IHF should do things for them. They want to see tangible things where for example, the efforts of the organisation results in the promotion of someone in the village to a better job.

Mr Winston Bacchus likes the fact that the Foundation is building stronger relationships with India. He thinks that India can help St. Vincent more in doing things such as funding a training institute. Mr Patrick Deane also thinks that the way forward is to strengthen relationships with India and with Indians and their organisations in regional territories. He thinks that St. Vincent should reach out to them and learn from those who are doing better.

Linking up with other organisations will enable us to achieve greater synergies. Technical and other resources can be shared and made available to sister organisations so that greater tangible results will be obtained from the current total resources in the region.

Analysing the stories and records for future use

CHAPTER 12

Verifying the Narratives

The stories presented by the interviewees were all tied together creating one chronological narrative starting with the arrival of the Indians to St. Vincent, their struggles on the estates, their movement from the estates demonstrating their survival strategies, their adjustments to life in a new society and their ambitions to attain better standards of living and lifestyles. However, there was little information from this set of interviewees about their ancestors in India and about the life of the indentured workers during the first fifty years (1861-1930) from the arrival of the first ship to St. Vincent. Mrs Jack, Mrs Bowman and Mrs Williams said they did not know anything about their ancestors from India nor much about life on the estates. Their stories were more about their personal lives and experiences. The others had a bit more recollection of the stories they heard of the lifestyles and conditions that existed prior to the 1930s.

In this chapter, there will be an analysis of the themes discussed in the interviews. The information will be compared with other sources available to give a fuller picture of the life of the Indians from the time they arrived in SVG to the present. The themes highlighted at the end of each interview falls into five broad timelines of about thirty or forty years which gives a better understanding of the chronology of the story of the Indians. There are overlaps of activities and conditions through different sections of this continuous timeline which documents the changes to and progress of the way of life of many Indians on the island.

1. From India to the Estates 1861- 1890

The stories of Rambaluck, and of Kalloo travelling from India with his family are substantiated in the ship lists of Indians that came to St. Vincent. The motivation to travel to another country must have been strong. Historical records show the famines in India and the British mismanagement of the agricultural economy were the main causes for Indians seeking better economic opportunities abroad. The promise of wages and a better life abroad must have been seen as a pot of gold but neither did they find that or a bed of roses in St. Vincent.

The ship's journeys themselves were terrible. Passengers were herded together and treated badly resulting in several deaths on the ships. On landing, some passengers had to wait at the depot in Kingstown with little comfort until they were allocated to the estates. Sometimes this waiting period was long and with only little help from the government, they suffered. Once on the estates, life was not easy. The overseers and planters who had just been denied the services of the African slaves continued treating the new workers as if they were slaves, in many respects.

According to the indentureship contracts, the Indians were to be paid wages (10 pence per day), given free housing which should be maintained by the planters, and given adequate medical services in exchange for their work on the estates over the period of 5 years and in later contracts, 3 or 4 years for those who agreed. In many instances the Indians were denied these contractual rights under various guises.

In some cases they were not provided with adequate medical services or facilities, their houses which would have been former barracks of the slaves were not properly maintained, some Indians were abused and wages were sometimes reduced. Women were also sometimes abused and denied adequate wages. As a result, some suffered hunger and malnutrition and became susceptible to diseases. These factors impacted the ability of the Indians to perform their tasks. With hungry bellies and illness many could not complete their tasks and were penalised further with reduction of their wages, which only exacerbated the problem. Many died on the estates from this treatment and from diseases such as yaws and dysentery.

Complaints for mistreatments and abuse had little redress as the magistrates often sided with the planters, their fellow British friends. Complaints and grievances often never got to the appropriate authority as restriction of movement and other means were used to prevent this. Actions taken by the Indians such as work to rule, was described as skulking and idleness by the planters and used as justification to reduce wages. As there was a gradual decrease in profitability of the sugar business over the indentureship period because of factors such as competition from the newly invented beet sugar in Europe and a better quality of sugar from other territories, the planters attempted to pass this economic loss to the indentured workers. More work was therefore demanded for less rewards. Wages were unlawfully reduced and other benefits of the workers were negatively impacted.

On a few occasions, groups of workers together protested their mistreatment. A protest of significance was a march from Argyle and Calder estates to Kingstown on October 7th, 1882 by several workers who claimed that they were not being allowed to return to India as per their contract. This resulted in the arrest and fine of seven Indians. However, they were later released after the appropriate government authorities got a better understanding of their plight and a decision was taken to finance the return to India of those who were not working. Many Indians therefore returned to India soon after. By 1885, nearly half of the Indians who came to St. Vincent had returned to India.

The last shipload of Indians who arrived in St. Vincent on the Lighting in 1880 would have served their five-year contracts by 1885 and any three-year renewal of contracts would have been completed before the early 1890s. The indenture-ship system was therefore effectively finished in SVG about 27 years before it was formally discontinued by the British in 1917. The remaining Indians in St. Vincent with little or no savings and no prospect of returning to India had to acclimatise into the wider society. They had already started to give up some of their culture and traditions while on the estates. For example, they christened their children with western names, and they joined Christian religions such as Wesleyan, Methodist, Anglican, and Catholicism.

Being only a small percent of the total population, changes to the wider community norms became easier. It is also reported that western names were required for registration in private primary schools and this could have been a factor for the Indians agreeing to christen their children using western names. There are other reports, such as that of Mr Walter Bacchus, in his interview, that some Indians grew to like the western names and voluntarily and willingly changed their names. The process of changing the names was done by baptism and christening and depending on the church at which this was done, the Indian would then be considered a member of that church.

2. From the Estates to village life 1890 - 1930

During the period 1890 to 1896 sugar exports of St. Vincent had dropped from £63,000 to £24,000 and total exports from £103,000 to £57,000. A Royal Commission of 1897 described the economy as being in "terminal decline and the majority of the population was enduring poverty. Sugar cane production was floundering because of poor land-management, pests, and poor processing and refining capacity. Arrowroot exports were suffering due to both a reduction in quality and over production and other economic crops (cocoa, fruit, spices, cotton) were produced in only small quantities". The hurricane of 1898 would have caused much damage to crops also.

A land settlement ordinance of January 1899 was therefore designed to help ex-slaves and Indians purchase their farm lands. £15,000 was given by the Colonial Office to purchase estate lands to be sold in five-acre allotments to applicants. The applicants were required to pay a deposit of 25% and the balance to be paid in 12 annual instalments starting five years later so that the total payment would be completed in about 16 years. Although the volcanic eruption of May 1902 to March 1903 would have delayed the implementation of this land settlement scheme, a few persons who had saved enough would have been able to purchase these lands.

As Mr Soleyn pointed out in his interview, some land owners wanted to sell their estates and return to Britain at this time. Some Indians were able to buy lands in areas which were good for housing and agriculture. In the period from leaving the estates in the 1890s to the 1930s some would have started to build wooden structures rather than wattle and daub houses. For example, the Indians from the Argyle estate bought land in Yambou, Akers, Calder, Glenside and Richland Park. The families in these villages had common ancestors in Argyle and were relatives.

A few also went to Trinidad, Aruba and other countries when it was possible to find work. Some stayed in these countries while others returned to St. Vincent. Around this time also, greater cultural shifts were occurring where they continued to give up their traditions and turn to different religions. Missionaries were active and they had a listening ear among some Indians.

3. Survival and Adaptation 1930 - 1960

During the next thirty years the cultural shifts continued. In Richland Park for example, there were a few conversions to the SDA church by the early 1930s which included Charles "Charlie" Thomas, the first leader of the church, James "Chowbow" Woods in 1831, Joseph Bacchus in 1935 and several (30) in 1938. The Seventh Day Adventist Church was established and in the next twenty years to 1960, most of the Indians in Richland Park had become Seventh Day Adventists. They had established a church by the early 1930s, a primary school in a house in 1935, and later a secondary school.

This conversion of the Indians led to a new way of life, where eating habits were changed, drinking of alcohol and wearing of jewellery were forbidden among other things. The lives of the Indians in Richland Park who joined the SDA church is an example of drastic change but Indians who joined other Christian religions in Richland Park and in other areas of SVG or did not join any religion at all, did not continue with many aspects of Hindu culture either. European dress and eating habits were adopted. The wearing of jewellery, although accepted by most Christian religions, decreased.

The plots of lands bought earlier were further divided as families multiplied. For example, in Richland Park, Rambaluck's son Rigley (Babu) divided up his lands among his children, Winston Bacchus and others. Kowlessur's son, Thomas "Seetaram" Woods who came from India at the age of 3 and later moved from Argyle to Richland Park, also divided his property among the next generation, James Woods and others. This happened in other areas of the country while other Indians nearer to estate lands that became available after the 1930s bought more land. Indians who had moved to villages nearby the Argyle estate for example were able to buy lands at Argyle.

The Indian population during this period increased immensely. A typical couple had between 7 and 14 children. Although several Indians migrated to Trinidad and later in the 1950s to the United Kingdom and the USA, the population of Indians would have increased by about ten times from 1900 to 1960.

During this time several Indians started various forms of businesses including grocery shops, passenger transport and small cottage industries, but most continued with their agricultural plots. Some tried their hands at the commercial production of cotton, cane, arrowroot and in the 1950s when banana production was introduced as the new cash crop a few also took up this offer.

4. More Comfortable Living 1960 - 1990

During this period the production of bananas flourished in St. Vincent. The Indians in the interior and the Windward areas of the country embarked heavily on the commercial production of bananas. Those who had bought virgin lands planted them with bananas. As the banana business rose from the 1960s, peaked in the 1980s and declined towards the end of the twentieth century, the fortunes of the farmers also rose and fell with it.

My family was intimately involved with this process. My uncle, Mr Donelly Bacchus, one of the pioneers of the banana industry in St. Vincent, encouraged other family members and villagers to get into the banana business. At one point, almost all of the agricultural lands in Richland Park were covered with bananas. The first banana station for buying and grading bananas in Richland Park was located at Monkey Hill. At that time the banana bunches were shipped to England on the stalk. I grew up in this period taking care of our several banana fields and selling the bananas at this station. Later Mr Donelly Bacchus, along with his brother Mr Vertyl Bacchus, three Indian brothers Alfonzo, Kenneth and Edward Lewis and Mr Henry (Cecil) Bailey established the first banana boxing plant in St. Vincent. This was at Kellipar, the northern area of Richland Park, on the way to Montreal.

Along with the improvements resulting from the banana industry, a few Indians were also involved in trade and light manufacturing but the real impetus for the upward mobility of the Indians in the next generations was through the improved education system in St. Vincent. In the case of Richland Park and surrounding villages, secondary education for most Indians was made possible via the SDA school, Mountain View Academy. The SDA church growth had skyrocketed among the Indians in Richland Park and among the wider population in SVG during this period so that it became a mainstream religion. Indian children were able to complete their high school education and either studied locally to become teachers or civil servants or go abroad to complete their tertiary education.

Many complete Indian family units also migrated in the 1970s and 1980s to find better opportunities. As Mr Winston Bacchus pointed out in his interview, subtle forms of racism existed in the government institutions, where the glass ceiling was harder to break for talented Indians. This factor along with the desire to find better economic and living spaces, motivated the Indians like others in the general population to migrate to cities like New York, Toronto and London. A few Indians who had put down roots abroad sold some of their properties but most held on to their properties in St. Vincent.

Both in SVG and abroad, some married within the Indian community whilst others married people from different ethnic backgrounds. Like others in the general population of SVG, they adapted to changes in village life where the next generations built bigger and more luxurious houses. Houses now were built of concrete, steel and galvanised roofs. They had indoor kitchens with stoves and fridges, and toilets with running water. Typically, there were two or three bedrooms, a living room and a garden. Some families had a motor vehicle and life was generally more comfortable than earlier years.

5. The Remnant 1990 - 2020

During the period 1990 to 2020, several of the Indians who remained in St. Vincent continued their upward mobility in housing and occupations while others did not. Some of the younger generations obtained employment in the public service and as teachers, but because of the relatively stagnant economy several migrated abroad. News of the economy in SVG could be one of the reasons why some who had moved abroad earlier also sold their properties in St. Vincent during this time. According to the CIA World Factbook of November 27th, 2020, based on 2012 estimates, only 1.1% (about 1,223 people) of the total population of SVG considered themselves to be Indian. This is a huge drop from the 6% of Indians reported to be in SVG prior to this period.

Of interest also, the CIA Factbook report states that as much as 23% of Vincentians considered themselves to be of a mixed race, whereas 71.2% were African descent, 3% Indigenous, 1.5% European and 2% other races. These statistics may demonstrate that there has been some more recent racial assimilation also among the Indians in SVG. Indians in SVG have now become a part of the melting pot of cultures. Like the "N" word, the "C" word is not used as often as when I was growing up as a young boy in the 1960s and 70s. There appears to be more tolerance for differences among ethnic groups.

All peoples are seen as equals with similar ambitions to have their children educated to the highest level, own property and have a good standard of living. The
formation of the SVG Indian heritage Foundation at the beginning of the twenty
first century was met with no resistance. The general population understands
that Indians are part of its life and culture. The support of both the two leading
political parties in SVG by unanimously approving the national recognition
of the Indian Arrival Day and Indian Heritage Day and other activities of the
Foundation demonstrates wide acceptance of the central role Indians played
and continues to play in the development of the country.

CHAPTER 13

A closer look at the records

During the time of the indentureship system the British kept several types of records. In the case of the workers who traveled to St. Vincent from India, records were produced both in India and St. Vincent. There are two sets of records that I found to be easily available. These are the Register of Indians at the National Archives in St. Vincent and the government of St. Vincent gazettes at the National Archives at Kew Gardens, London. There are several other types of records pertaining to the Indians both in St. Vincent and the UK. In India also there should be copies of several records pertaining to the indentured workers who travelled to St. Vincent to work.

In India, each indentured worker was inspected and issued a certificate that they were fit for work. Copies of the ship manifest listing the Indian passengers should also be in India. Each passenger was also given an immigration pass, copies of which should be both in India and St. Vincent. However, I have not been able to verify if these records in particular still exist in India. In St. Vincent there should also be copies of the government gazettes for the period and other records, which as yet I have not been able to find. I was told of church records in St. Vincent which I tried to find but was unable to access. There is therefore a need to spend more resources and time to search to see if more records are available.

In most cases special permission will need to be obtained from the various holders of these documents. This process to access and study the various documents in India, St. Vincent and the UK to gather more data and a more thorough history of the Indians who travelled to St. Vincent will require appropriate financing, time, effort and the cooperation of several entities. Further research projects will bring immense benefit to the people of St. Vincent, India, the Indo-Vincentian diaspora and others.

In this chapter therefore, we shall look at some of the samples of the available records of the life and movement of the Indians and demonstrate the importance and shortcomings of some of these records. In chapter 14 we shall discuss how these records can be used to reconnect Indo-Vincentians with India and vice versa. Below, therefore are some samples of the records that we have with a commentary about each. There are also a few documents from other territories that are unavailable or absent in St. Vincent which could have been beneficial. Appendix I, II and III provide more samples of some documents discussed in this chapter. These are pages of the register of Indians, copies of pages of the gazettes and spreadsheets of the information from these sources.

Register of Indians

I encountered the Register of Indians at the old National Archives building at Frenches, Kingstown in the early 1990s when I was searching for information about the Indians of SVG. Several years later on July 20th, 2006, at the first formal launching of the SVG IHF at Pitani Resort Argyle, this register was presented to the Foundation by the then Honourable Minister of Urban Development, Culture, Labour and Electoral Matters, Mrs Rene Baptiste. At the launching Mr Kahnai Kangal of the Trinidad Indo-Caribbean Cultural Centre was present and was delighted to see this important book. Below is a picture of the SVG Register of Indians.

Since then this register has had much more traffic to its pages and its condition has deteriorated but with the building of the new National Archives, it has found a better place of display and handling. Its contents have been photographed and made available online so that physical handling is now not very necessary. Below is a copy of the first two pages of the register. Clearer copies of samples of these pages can be viewed in Appendix 1.

This register lists the names of the passengers who travelled from India on the eight ships from 1861 to 1880. As can be seen in the first column of the sample page, each passenger was given a unique colonial or registration number which runs from 1 to 2746. After the number 1240 a few entries (1241-1250) were erased and the numbering continued from 1550. There are a few registration numbers that are either void or with no information in the row. One name was usually written for each passenger but in a few cases, a second name or surname was written. Passengers were also assigned a ship number for the particular ship they travelled on. The names of family members are usually consecutive in the ship numbers. The age, sex, height, birthplace in India, father's name and any distinguishing body marks were generally given. Money advanced (for the ship's fare) to be repaid out of wages and other notes about the passengers were written on the second page of each entry.

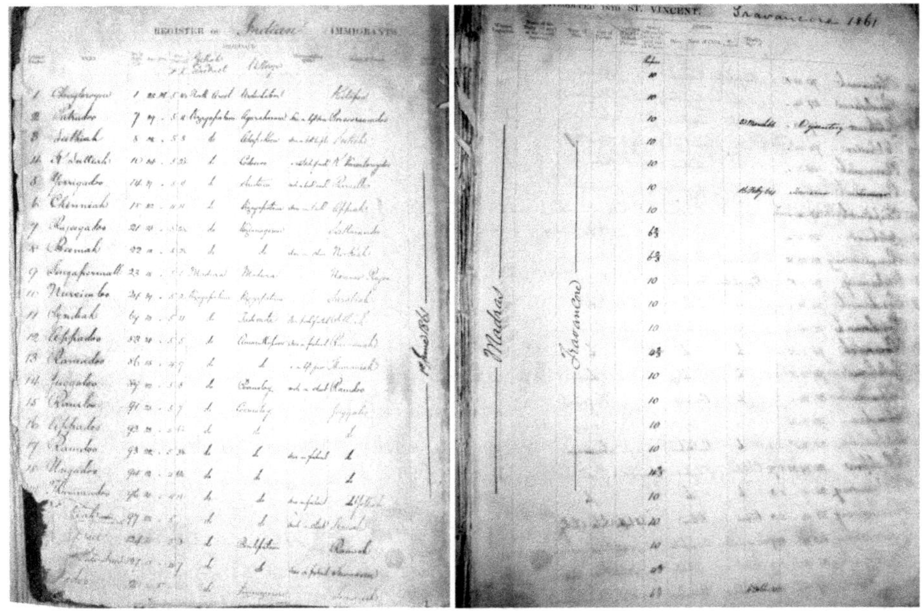

Please see Appendix I for more samples of these pages. On several pages of the register the birthplace information is missing. The castes of the Indians were not written for any of the passengers in this register although caste is identified on records of indentured Indians in some other British territories. Many of the names in the register seem to have been written as they sound in English and would likely have a different spelling in India. The birthplace for several passengers is also missing and have not been recorded for three of the seven ships.

All the information from this register was copied to spreadsheets by Mr Cheddie Richards of St. Lucia. Please see samples of these in Appendix II. I am assisting the SVG IHF in upgrading these spreadsheets with additional information from other records with the aim of eventually making them available to the public.

Gazette pages

In addition to the register of Indians, the gazettes of the government of St. Vincent hold a wealth of information on various topics including those related to the Indians. For example, they list the passengers from India by ships, by dates contracted and by estates allocated. However, information about passengers' addresses in India and caste are also missing from these records. Some ship lists are also missing but for those that are available, the names of the estates to which the Indians were allocated in St. Vincent, are documented. See Appendix III for samples of these gazette pages.

Immigration Pass

The following is an example of an Immigration pass that was issued in India for each indentured worker before they left. This copy for a male Indian to Guyana is credited to Mr Asne K. Rajpal of the International Foundation for Vedic Science, Ontario N6C 4Z1 who shared it in a presentation by the Indo-Caribbean Cultural Centre on February 7th, 2021.

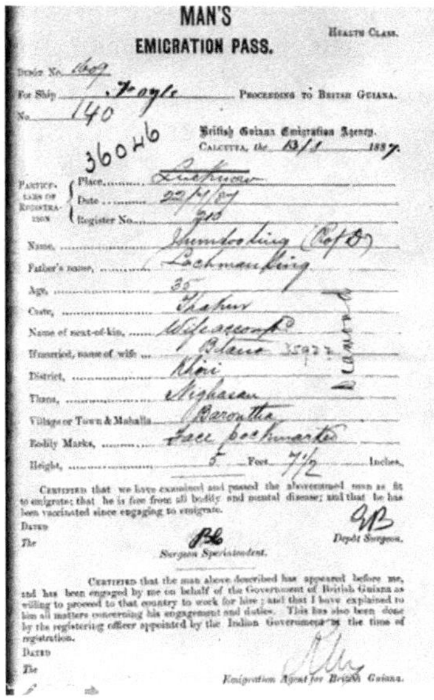

Unfortunately, none of these passes have been found in St. Vincent. Most of the information on these however are also written in the register of Indians in St. Vincent. Two pieces of vital information on this form, the caste of the worker and his district thana or police station in India are however missing from the Indian register in St. Vincent.

These words are written at the bottom of the pass: "Certified that we have examined and passed the above-named man as fit to immigrate; that he is free from all bodily and mental disease; and that he has been vaccinated since engaging to emigrate." Signed by the Surgeon Superintendent and the Depot Surgeon.

The Emigration Agent also signed below the following note: "Certified that the man above described has appeared before me and has been engaged by me on behalf of the Government of British Guiana as willing to proceed to that country to work for hire; and that I have explained to him all matters concerning his engagement and duties. This has also been done by the registering officer appointed by the Indian government at the time of registration". Emigration passes were also issued for women.

There are other records scattered at different locations that can be used to reconstruct the story of the Indians of St. Vincent. Some of these include the records of baptism at various churches, records of birth, marriage, land ownership or deeds, wills and death records. Some of the places these records are kept are at the Government Registry in Kingstown, the Mt. Coke Church near Calder, and other churches in Mesopotamia, Georgetown, Kingstown and on the Leeward side of the Island. A project spearheaded by the SVG IHF with the cooperation of the government of St. Vincent and the Grenadines with funding from interested donor agencies can have all or most of these documents scanned and further digitised and held in an approved section of the National Archives of

SVG. This will aid in the preservation of the records. If they are made available online, this will limit physical handling and will also aid access to researchers globally.

Example of Family Tree

This is my family tree up to the Indians that came on the ships. Some of the information is still missing and some of it has to be verified. If other records are obtained, I, along with other people of SVG Indian heritage, will be able to add to family trees, which in turn may broaden the trees of families in India and other territories. All those ancestors whose names are in the outer arch of my family tree below, travelled from India to St. Vincent.

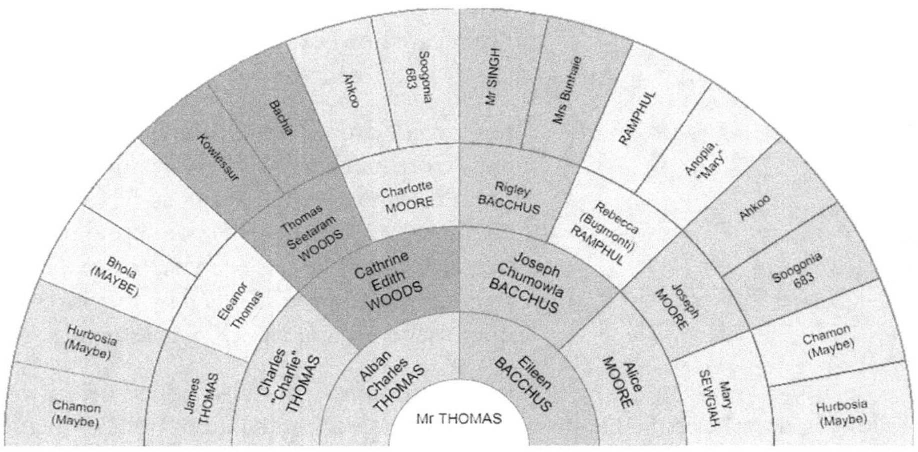

CHAPTER 14

Reconnecting families in the diaspora and India

Many Vincentians of Indian Heritage have been thinking of reconnecting with their families in India. Several have constructed family trees and some have linked their families to the passengers that came on the ships from India. Although a few have also been to India as tourists, in recent times as it has become more financially possible, none has yet indicated that they have linked up with their families in India. I have been working on linking up with my family in India since 2007 when I went on a course in Hyderabad, India. In this chapter, I will share some of my experience in this search and explain some of the best methods we can use, having also listened to and consulted with some of the best Indian genealogists and researchers in the Caribbean region.

I was able to visit Varanasi (Benares) at the end of the course in 2007, for one day in an effort to visit the family address of my maternal great great grandfather Rambaluck, that I had found written in the Register of Indian as Pasoree, Chanowlee, Benares. I enjoyed the tourist attractions of Varanasi, going on the Ganges and witnessing the evening celebrations from the gnats. However, the village of Pasoree was not to be found. Several things have changed since our ancestors left India over a century and a half ago and there is a need to look at the records more closely.

I have since discovered that the names of some villages in India have changed, or combined with other villages or even incorporated into larger towns or cities. The name of the village, Pasoree, may have also been misspelled by the British clerks who entered it into the records. The district of Chanowlee seems to actually be the district of Chandauli which has since been separated from Varanasi some years ago. There are about four villages in Chandauli, which could be possible candidates for Pasoree. None is spelt that way but there are some that have similarity in phonetics. These are some of the problems that would be encountered when searching for the family of our ancestors in India.

Before going to India to search for your ancestors, therefore, it is advisable to do as much prior research as possible, to identify any possible families there. The most important information to get is the birthplace of your ancestors in India and the name of any relatives who remained in India at the time of departure over one hundred years ago. Other records in India can be used to trace any present-day family of that ancestor and the location of the ancestor's birthplace and current family addresses. Similarly, relatives in India can use the records in India and St. Vincent to trace their family living in St. Vincent and the diaspora.

In St. Vincent one of the main sources of information is from oral stories passed down by family members, and others, as mentioned in Chapter 13, are the register of Indians, birth and baptismal records at the churches, marriage and death certificates. The caste of the Indians are missing from the records in St. Vincent and though not as important in St. Vincent, this is very important in finding your family in India. The families in India still adhere to the caste system and live according to those classifications.

The information about caste can be sourced from stories passed down by the older family members. For example, in my family tree, an older family member, Mr Peter Moore said that the Moore family were Brahmins. Therefore, the father of the Moore family, Ahkoo, who came from India, would have been Brahmin, the caste of priests and scholars. Mr Peter Moore also said that Rambaluck, who also came from India, was a Ksatrya and a pundit. However, as you also read in the interview with Mr Walter Bacchus, he said that Rambaluck was a Raj, or Prince of high status in India who was kidnapped and brought to St. Vincent. Both Ahkoo and Rambaluck are on my maternal side.

My paternal grandmother's brother James Chowbow Woods said that his grandfather, Kowlessur, was from a tribe who looked after cattle. The cattle herders, farmers, traders and artisans were Vaishyas. Whereas, comments from John Thomas, son of James Thomas, my paternal great grandfather of Richland Park and others from the family suggest that they were Brahims. Another elder family member, Mr Peter Moore supported this too by saying that James "Pa Thomas was also a Brahmin..." The correct information about caste could be vital in identifying families in India. However, if the caste is not known in SVG and the relative is found in India, the caste will be discovered.

Many Indians in St. Vincent and the diaspora who now use western names do not know their original Indian surnames. This will therefore have to be verified by looking at the records of christening and baptism at the churches and any other relevant records at the government registry. Once the Indian name is known, you will have to look at the register of Indians to find that name. The name may be spelt differently but the phonetic sound is usually similar. For example, the ancestor of the Cordice family is known to be Satoo, but in the Register of Indians, it is Sahatoo. On the other hand, names may be spelt incorrectly in the register of Indians. For example, Rambaluck is written in the register but the correct spelling may be Ram Balak.

Once the name is identified in the register of Indians, the row should show the name of the father and the place of birth in India. Unfortunately, this information is missing for three of the eight ships from India and for a few names on the other ships. The birthplaces and some father's names are missing for all passengers on the Countess of Ripon of 1866. Some of the passengers' ages, father's names and birthplace are missing on the Emperatice Eugenie of 1869. The birthplace is missing for all of the passengers on the Lightning of 1880. Unless duplicate records of the missing information are found in India or other locations, you will not be able to identify father's names or birthplaces in India. However, if the father's name and birthplace in India is found, the search can then move to the records in India.

Mr Shamsun Deen of Trinidad, has assisted many people in searching for and finding their relatives in India, including former Prime Ministers of Trinidad and Tobago, Mr Basdeo Pandy and Ms Kamla Persad-Bissessar. I have listened to his presentations on Zoom Indo-Caribbean Cultural Centre Programs, looked at excerpts of his book, Lineages & Linkages, Solving Trinidad Roots in India, and held several conversations with him and would like to acknowledge his input regarding the following information.

Mr Deen said that there are copies in India of the records of the indentured Indians who migrated to various overseas territories. These could be found at the Indian National Archives at Lucknow, Bihar, Delhi and other places. Additional records for Muslims can also be found at the Hajj centres in Mumbai and also at the Aligarh Muslim University. There are also Pariwar registers which are family registers in the villages themselves and Pharders which are Hindu ancestry records in cities such as Paranar, Varanasi and Gaya.

However, one of the best offices to assist you in finding your family in India after you have identified the address of your ancestor's birthplace and father's name, is the Office of the District Magistrate. It is advisable to have a letter from St. Vincent's National Archives or from someone of authority in the government of SVG for easier access as the records to be searched in India are legal documents.

Once the District Magistrate office authorises the search, you will be able to access the smaller District Records Centers or record rooms called collectorate or Kachari. Some of the documents that can be obtained here to find your family in India are the land registers (Khatauni), the death registers and the electoral rolls for villages. The voters' lists were kept from 1852 when the first elections were held in India and families were kept in blocks. The death registers started from 1897 and have father's names that stretch a lifespan earlier. Following is a quote from page 160 of Mr Deen's book, Lineages and Linkages showing the process of how the land records and Death Register can be used to assist with your search.

Once you have discovered the names and address of your cousins, you can head to the village with the records in hand. In these villages the caste system is strongly adhered to and you will need to find the people of your caste, especially the elders. Be aware that there may be people who may want to claim you as their family to see what they can get from you. Be aware also that some people in the villages still suffer from "recruiter phobia" where they may think that you are coming to take their children or members of their family. There is also a fear of losing their property and they may wonder why a long lost, distant family is interested in finding them. Are they coming to claim our property? Some Muslim families are also fearful to give info because of new laws being passed in India. They fear that they may suffer discrimination and other ills. Some families also think that their ancestors only went to Calcutta and would be shocked to learn or may not want to believe that they went to distant lands overseas.

It is therefore recommended that enough time is planned to be able to visit the family on more than one occasion. This will remove any hesitancy and fear and could lead to the building of new and fruitful relationships.

The above process was described for descendants of Indentured workers who wish to find their family in India but the reverse process, with the same documents can be used by Indians in India who want to find their families abroad.

CHAPTER 15

SVG Indian Heritage Foundation

In this chapter I will briefly review the new interest in the motherland, India and summarize some of the activities and achievements during the development of the SVG Indian Heritage Foundation over the past sixteen years. Below is an account of the formation of the Foundation, written in 2007, which gives a brief summary of its activities from inception to 2007 when I travelled abroad. Following this account, I shall give some more details of these activities and those of subsequent years.

"The SVG Indian Heritage Foundation was formed at a chance gathering of a few Vincentians of Indian origin at Indian Bay on August 16, 2005 when family members visited the Baptiste home. Present were Lenroy Thomas, Lucel Thomas, Deniston Bacchus, Denzil Bacchus and members of the Baptiste family including Osley Baptiste, Elvira Baptiste, Anna Insanali and Veda Scully. Destiny must have brought the group together on that historic occasion as no one had planned to meet there on that eventful day for that purpose. When I brought up the idea of forming an Indian organization, everyone present exploded with the same desire for this to be a reality.

The formation of an organization to advance the cause of the East Indians in St. Vincent and the Grenadines (SVG) must have been on the hearts of many Indo-Vincentians over the years. Several people may have thought about the idea and considered the advantages of having such an organization formed. I have been told that attempts were made as early as the 1960s by people such as Mr Donelly Bacchus and later by Mr Osley Baptiste to establish an entity with focus on the Indians of SVG.

The formation of the Indo-Vincentian group by Mrs Leah Bacchus in North America must also be given credit for its work in its effort to bring the Indians of SVG together. However, it was only until August 16, 2005 at 6:00 pm that firm actions were taken to establish an organization for the Indians of SVG and those in the Diaspora.

The impromptu meeting at Indian Bay later got structured and the name "SVG Indian Heritage Foundation" was proposed. We later had a "brain-storming" session where we discussed what should be the purpose of the Foundation. Many ideas were put forward including: the apparent lack of a strong identity of Vincentian children overseas; the history of the Indians in SVG; genealogy; efforts to start Indian Associations in the past; cultural affiliation and exchanges with regional

Indian organizations; establishing Indo-Vincentians chapters overseas; the Hindu religion; the exchange of information etc. One of the most significant ideas that came out of the meeting was that the new organization should place great emphasis on the sharing of pertinent information such as our history and genealogy among Indians both in SVG and in the Diaspora.

The meeting agreed to take action to have the name of the new organization registered as a "not-for-profit" entity. It was agreed that the formation of the organization should be published and a suitable venue should be sorted for a general meeting. An advertisement was therefore placed in the Searchlight newspaper, which brought attention to the formation of the group.

A few months later I was contacted by the editor of the Searchlight newspaper who wanted to feature the different cultural groups of SVG in the Searchlight issue during the week in which National Heroes Day (March 14) was celebrated. On that occasion therefore an article about the East Indians of SVG was featured in the Searchlight of March 17, 2006 which generated a stir in the minds of the people of SVG and abroad and created a huge response by several members of the Indian community and also initiated wider National discussion. A subsequent article invited the public's "…ideas, suggestions and contributions".

Interest was therefore generated in SVG and in the Diaspora and later a lecture was presented by Vincentian Indian historian, Dr Arnold Thomas at the UWI on June 1, 2006. Additional members of the Indian community became involved and after further outdoor activities at Argyle and informal meetings an official meeting was held at the Pitani Resort, Argyle on July 20, 2006 where the first formal Executive of the SVG Indian Heritage Foundation was elected. The SVG IHF therefore began its task of representing and catering for the needs of the Indo-Vincentian community.

The passing of an Act on March 26, 2007 by the Parliament of St. Vincent and the Grenadines to recognize June 1st as Indian Arrival Day and October 7 as SVG Indian Heritage Day was one of the most significant accomplishments of the SVG IHF. However, of interest also are the other important events of the Foundation's early years."

The early years of the Foundation were exciting ones where history was created for the Indians of SVG having had legislation passed in Parliament about them in particular. The last legislation which focused on the Indians of SVG would have been more than a hundred years previously. So the generations living at the beginning of the twenty-first century would have never heard the government discussing any topic related to the Indians of SVG, specifically. Mention must be made of some of the persons who were instrumental in propelling the early movement of the Foundation to achieve its successes.

There are several persons who shaped the way forward for the organisations holding regular meetings at Mr Osley Baptiste house, Macedonia Rock Hotel, the Helping Hands building in New Montrose, and residences in other areas of St. Vincent. Persons on the committees in the early days included Mr Lenroy Thomas, Mr Denzil Bacchus, Mr Osley Baptiste, Mr Noel Bacchus, Ms Janice Deane, Mr Branson Thomas, Mr Elmore Gaymes, Mrs Cheryl Rodriguez, Mr Junior Bacchus, Mrs Anna Insanali neé Baptiste, Mr Hannif Sutherland, Dr Junior Bacchus and Mrs Glenda Joyette. Appendix IV is a copy of the registration document of the Foundation which shows the members of the first formal committee but there were several others who contributed to the formation of the organisation.

Dr Arnold Thomas who had done extensive research on the Indians of St. Vincent also played a significant role in sensitising the public with his articles, presentations and liaising with officials from the Governments of SVG and India and with Indian organisations such as GOPIO, the Global Organisation of People of Indian Origin and the NCIC, National Council of Indian Culture in Trinidad and Tobago. He, along with Mr Branson Thomas also supported and propelled the organisation especially in the communities of Calder and Argyle.

The Honourable Rene Baptiste, previous minister of Culture of the government of SVG also played an important role in the Foundation's relationship with the government and has been supporting it since its launch. She was also the Parliamentarian who moved the motion to have the Act to recognize Indian Arrival Day passed on March 26, 2007. She was at Argyle earlier when the first formal Executive Committee was selected and symbolically presented the Register of Indians to the Foundation. She was also given the privilege of honouring some members of the Foundation with commemorative pins.

Mr Hanif Sutherland who arranged to have these pins made was also the designer of the logo of the Foundation. He also provided the technical services in setting up the first Website of the Foundation in 2006-2007 with Mr Lenroy Thomas and himself as administrators and forum moderators. Mr Lenroy Thomas and others in the diaspora later set up a Facebook group which lasted ten years until a new website was set up with the assistance of Mr Noel Thomas. A new Facebook page and group have since been set up by the website team, managed by Mr Lenroy Thomas, Mr Noel Thomas and Mr Colvin Harry.

The support of Mr Khani Kangal, President of the National Council of Indian Culture in Trinidad and Tobago must also be mentioned. At the first opportunity, he accepted to assist the Foundation. He was there for its launch and took pride in seeing the St. Vincent's Register of Indians highlighted for the first time. Over the years he was instrumental in sending various cultural groups, dancers and resource personnel to St. Vincent and would be present for important functions of the Foundation.

Over the last sixteen years, the Foundation has made several strides under the leadership of four presidents, namely Mr Elmore Gaymes, Dr Junior Bacchus, Mr Hansby King and Mr Junior Bacchus. In addition to those achievements mentioned above, the Foundation established a formal relationship with the government of India. The Minister of Overseas Affairs of India, Vayalar Ravi visited SVG on the occasion of the celebration of Indian Arrival Day on June 1, 2007. This was a significant event as no Minister of the Indian government had ever visited SVG before. The Honorary Consul of India to SVG, Mr Junior Bacchus was appointed in 2020, also a first.

The Foundation has hosted other Indian officials in SVG, hosted annual Yoga classes, annual Indian Arrival Days, Annual Indian Heritage Days and the first International India Diaspora Conference was held in SVG on June 1-3, 2012. It has also facilitated visits to schools giving cultural presentations. It has conducted negotiations with the government of SVG on behalf of members of the Indian community.

The current Executive Committee of the Foundation is as follows: President, Mr Junior Bacchus; First Vice President, Mr Dave Baptiste; Secretary and Website Administrator, Mrs Luann Hadaway; Vice President, Culture, Mr Denzil Bacchus; Vice President, Regional Coordinator, Mr Laurel Thomas; Assistant Secretary, Mrs Anna Insanali (Baptiste); Treasurer, Mrs Cheryl Rodriguez; Public Relations Officer and Website Administrator (SVG), Colvin Harry. Overseas Website and Facebook Administrators are Mr Noel Thomas, Mr Lenroy Thomas and Mr Shawn Bullock.

As stated on its website, the Foundation was *"...formed to represent the interest of the East Indian community of SVG and those in the diaspora. It aims to instil a greater sense of pride in our heritage and culture. It seeks to create opportunities for Indo-Vincentians to learn more about and preserve their history, to create and strengthen relationships and to improve all other aspects of the Indian community."* The Foundation has made monumental progress in the last sixteen years. In the next chapter we shall look at the possibilities for greater progress.

Following are pictures of some of the events of the Foundation over the last fifteen years.

Indian Arrival Day Re enactment at Indian Bay on various occasions

Ambassador of India Mahendra Singh Kanyal and spouse visit SVG

21.2.19 Musicians from India perform at Russell's Auditorium

15.1.18 Donation of cash to purchase chicken feed for its school programme to Calder Government School on its 60th anniversary

16.2.18 SVG Indian Heritage Foundation's Day at the Calder Government School on its 60th anniversary. The Foundation provided Indian lunch for all teachers, parents, students and visitors. Mr Purushottam Singh of Trinidad and Tobago brought an Indian dancer to perform. Mr Elmore Gaymes taught Yoga and Mrs Cheryl Rodriguez led modelling in her Indian sari while students and teachers modeled outfits provided by the Foundation.

16.2.18 President Mr Junior Bacchus and Treasurer Mrs Cheryl Rodriguez met with the Headmaster to plan SVG IHF's Day during the 60th anniversary celebrations and were presented with commemorative polo shirts

13.1.19 SVF IHF Executive Committee meeting at Mrs Anna Insanali's residence at Indian Bay, the house where the Foundation had its first meeting.

8.6.19 Secretary Mrs Luann Hadaway presented a plaque to Mr Purushottam Singh of T&T, whom the Executive honoured for his contribution to all events over the years.

23.6.19 Members of the SVG IHF Executive joined Denzil to celebrate his birthday in Montreal, Richland Park

04.06.19 Indian Arrival Day. SVG IHF Executive worshipped at the Calder Seventh Day Adventist Church

07.09.18 The Executive attended Danielle Baptiste's wedding

02.03.20 Executive met with Dr Hon. Ralph E. Gonsalves
Prime Minister of SVG at Cabinet Room

10.03.20 President, Junior and Treasurer, Cheryl met with H.E. Cenio Lewis,
High Commissioner of SVG to the U.K. at the Ministry of Foreign Affairs.

October 2019 Visit to Richland Park on a scenic drive with the Embassy
of India, Suriname's Rep. to Independence celebrations in SVG.

02.06.19 IAD Rally and honouring ceremony at Rawacou

Honouring of Mr Kahnai Kangal of the NCIC of Trinidad & Tobago

SVG Indian Heritage Foundation

10.09.19 Prime Minister Dr the Hon. Ralph E. Gonsalves, and his delegation on his official visit to India meeting Prime Minister Mahendra Modi of India

10.09.19 Prime Minister Dr the Hon. Ralph E. Gonsalves, on his official visit to India, presented Cheryl, the SVG IHF Executive's representative, to Prime Minister Mahendra Modi of India

10.09.19 Dr The Hon. Ralph Gonsalves, Prime Minister of SVG meets Shri. Narendra Modi, Prime Minister of India

09.09.19 SVG Delegation at Conference and 10.09.19 Dinner in India

03.09.20 Ceremony of President Junior's appointment as Hon. Council for India to SVG and handing over of medical supplies at Murray's Height Hotel

22.10.19 SVG IHF Executive visit to Diwali celebrations, Chaguanas, Trinidad

Photos from various events of the SVG IHF

CHAPTER 16

The Way Forward

We have seen through the pages of this book the long history that exists between St. Vincent and the Grenadines and India. June 1ˢᵗ, 2021 marked the 160ᵗʰ anniversary of the arrival of the first Indians to St. Vincent. The Indians have struggled, survived, lived fairly comfortably and excelled in a foreign land. They have proved to be ambitious, adventurous and generally prefer to keep active, moving forwards and upwards. They have expanded into a wider diaspora of Europe, North America and other countries. They have developed a unique cultural identity during their sojourn. The time has therefore come for hands to be stretched out to clasp with others for further progress and greater developments such as in the economic and cultural spheres.

As highlighted in chapter 15, several things were accomplished for the people of SVG since the establishment of the SVG IHF. Officials from India, including a government minister, have visited SVG. We have developed close and better relationships with the government of India and its embassy in Suriname. Persons from SVG have been to India on courses. A delegation from SVG, with the highest official in SVG, the Prime Minister, Dr The Honourable Ralph Gonsalves has visited India in an official capacity. An Honorary Consul of India, Mr Junior Bacchus, has been appointed to St. Vincent and the Grenadines. The government of India has made several donations to assist various projects in SVG, most recently the donation of 40,000 doses of vaccines to combat the Covid 19 virus.

The time is therefore right for a quantum leap in the relationship between these two countries. What are the strengths and opportunities of these countries and how can these be used to foster the betterment of the people in both countries? Are there current opportunities in trade, education, health, agriculture, manufacturing, international relations, cultural exchanges and tourism for example, that can add value to both countries? Are there ways that Indo-Vincentians could be better represented in SVG and abroad? These are questions that require in-depth analysis that would be very helpful to both the people of India and SVG. Below, however, I will only summarise some pertinent data about India and SVG and suggest some progressive possibilities.

According to investindia.gov.in, 2020, India is the World's seventh largest economy and has the third largest purchasing power in the World. It is the second most populous country in the World with a population of 1.4 billion. Its travel and tourism market is worth US$ 475 billion. Its commerce market is worth US $100 billion. Its top performing sectors are agriculture, industry, services, food processing and manufacturing. Its economy has been growing aggressively and is projected to continue steady growth. India is targeting a $5 trillion economy by 2030 with a growth rate of 8%. St. Vincent and the Grenadines on the other hand is a small country that can fit into a corner of a rural district in India. With a population of just over a hundred thousand and an economy of about US$0.4 billion, it is miniscule when compared to India. However, further benefits can be gained by both countries with the deepening of relationships.

There may be possibilities for India to assist SVG in agriculture and agro processing not only by financing projects such as the arrowroot industry or in giving aid in times of disasters but also by providing technical assistance and equipment. India has expertise in the field of agriculture and agro processing that can be very vital to the development of these sectors in SVG. India has also developed various types of processing and agricultural equipment that can assist in cottage industries and small-scale industrial production of juices, condiments and starches. Potential crops are cassava, arrowroot, corn, turmeric, pepper, mushrooms and fruits among others. Successful implementation of these projects can add tremendous value to the Vincentian economy.

Trade with India has traditionally been hampered by the distance and the resultant high cost of freight. There have also been language barriers. However, these obstacles are now diminishing because of the proliferation of English and the development of Hinglish in India. Communication with English speaking countries is therefore better facilitated. The lower cost of labour, economies of scale, specialist assets, lower currency among other factors have made goods from India more competitive in western countries. Medicine is now imported by the West from India. Textiles, iron, steel and paper have been imported by SVG from India. Indian online services are also used globally. There are therefore greater possibilities of doing business with India, especially the importation of industrial equipment and specialist services.

Strengthening diplomatic relationships between India and SVG also has advantages. For example, having a common position on a matter of international implications can also be beneficial when negotiating within the international community. SVGs' vote could be very valuable to India and vice versa.

There are several Indo-Vincentians both in SVG and in the diaspora who are interested in finding their ancestors' family and villages in India and who would like to experience life as a tourist in India. If the arrangements are made to facilitate easier online genealogy research, and travel restrictions are removed, more people will be able to find the villages in India from which their ancestors originate. Tours from Canada, the USA, England and the Caribbean can be set up for Indo-Vincentians to visit these villages and also to do sightseeing. This would not only be enjoyed by Indo-Vincentians but the economy of India will benefit from this form of genealogical tourism.

There can also be tours and projects for Indians from India to visit SVG. Indians who can afford the trip may also want to visit the land to which their ancestors migrated. Specialist workers in India who can provide technical assistance to SVG would also enjoy participating in short-term projects in SVG, enjoying the new environment while contributing to the development of SVG. SVG has a rich resource of clean, natural beauty. There are lovely beaches with clear water in St. Vincent and in the Grenadines. These high-quality beaches are not easy to find in Asia.

SVG has already benefited from visiting cultural groups from India and other Caribbean territories. A musical group performed in SVG and tutoring of Yoga has been conducted by personnel from India. These types of cultural exchanges should be encouraged and developed further.

As a further attraction to visitors and for the benefit of future generations, the rich cultural history and heritage of the Indians of SVG needs to be preserved. All historical records pertaining particularly to the Indians of SVG should be properly digitised, stored and made available online to the general public. One possible site is at the National Archives. Another recommendation is to establish a museum to house samples of records pertaining to the Indians, implements and other artifacts used by the indentured workers and their descendants in SVG. This could be housed in an appropriate area where the Indians lived, such as Argyle, Richland Park or Calder.

Following are the pictures of two items that are very valuable to the Indians of SVG that could be housed in this museum if they can be obtained from Barbados. A request should be made to the government of Barbados to deliver these to the SVG IHF. If they cannot be obtained, all efforts should be made to ensure that they are secured and displayed to the public by an appropriate facility of the government of Barbados. These items, a ship bell and a barometer were salvaged from the Countess of Ripon, which sank off the South West coast of Barbados on January 20th, 1866. This ship was carrying Indians bound for St. Vincent and Grenada. All passengers were saved and they continued their onward journey to St. Vincent on the HMS Wolverine.

Implementation of suggestions like those mentioned above will enhance the image of SVG globally and bring economic benefits to its citizens.

Book References, Links & Places Visited

Anderson, Robert M., 1938, The Handbook of St. Vincent, Office of the "Vincentian", Kingstown St. Vincent

Bailey, George, 2012, The Valley, Asquith Bailey, 33 Shorebreeze Court, East Palo Alto CA 94303, (Life in Marriaqua 1930 - 60)

Britanica Academic, St. Vincent and the Grenadines, https://academic-eb-com.eres.qnl.qa/levels/collegiate/article/Saint-Vincent-and-the-Grenadines/117397

Burton, William, 6th December, 2015, The Wreck of the SV Countess of Ripon, https://www.bajanthings.com/shipwreck-sv-countess-of-ripon/

Collins, Larry, 1975, Freedom at Midnight, Simon and Schuster, New York, USA

Dash, Mike, 2012, https://www.smithsonianmag.com/history/pass-it-on-the-secret-that-preceded-the-indian-rebellion-of-1857-105066360/

Deen, Shamshu, 1998, Lineages & Linkages, Solving Trinidad Roots in India, Printed by Print and Art Services Chaguanas, Trinidad and Tobago

Deen, Shamshu, Rajpal, Asne K. & Hassankhan, Maurits, Jan 3rd and Feb 7th 2021, Indo-Caribbean Cultural Centre Zoom Programs - Parts 1 & 2 & 3

Emmer, PC., 1986, The meek Hindu; the recruitment of Indian indentured labourers for service overseas, 1870-1916, Springer and Dordrecht ttps://link.springer.com/chapter/10.1007%2F978-94-009-4354-4_9

Encyclopaedia Britannica, https://www.britannica.com/place/Saint-Vincent-and-the-Grenadines/History

Huggins, Stephen, 2007 , Contributions to SVG IHF Forum , Retrieved from archives of www.svgihf.com

Immigration Office of St. Vincent, Register of Immigrants No 1, Indians, 1861-1880, National Archives, St. Vincent and the Grenadines

Julian, Richard, 2010, "Pigmented Spectacles." Conversations with Dr Ian Ayrton Earle Kirby Can Vet J.

Mahabir, Kumar, 1982, An interview with a 93-year old Indian, Mr James Woods of St. Vincent, Race retention and culture loss: South Asians/East Indians in St. Vincent, dmahabir@gmail. com and mahab@tstt.net

Marshall, Peter, 2011, King's College, London Universityhttp://www.bbc.co.uk/history/british/victorians/indian_rebellion_01.shtml

McNamara, Robert, June 30, 2018, A Timeline of India in the 1800, ThoughtCo., https://www.thoughtco.com/timeline-of-india-in-the-1800s-1774016

Patel, Dinyar, 2016, https://www.bbc.com/news/world-asia-india-36339524

Richards, Cheddie & Thomas, Lenroy, 2018, Spreadsheet copy of St. Vincent Indian Ship lists, Shared privately to selected researchers but yet to be published.

St. Vincent Gazettes, CO264/9-12, 1868-1880, National Archives, Kew Gardens, London

Searchlight Newspaper, Editor Claire Keizer, March 30, 2007, Indian Arrival Day Act Passed. (Acknowledgement of article and photo)

Stone, Linda S., 1973), "East Indian Adaptations on St. Vincent: Richland Park". University of Massachusetts - Amherst, Report 12: Windward Road: Contributions to the Anthropology of St. Vincent Anthropology Department Research Reports series

SVG Indian Heritage Facebook Group Forum, 2010

SVG Indian Heritage Foundation Facebook Group Forum, 2021

SVG IHF Website, 2021, www.svgihf.org

SVG IHF Website Forum, 2007, Retrieved from archives of www.svgihf.com

Siddiqui, Kalim, 2020, https://worldfinancialreview.com/the-political-economy-of-famines-during-the-british-rule-in-india-a-critical-analysis/

Tinker, H, 1993, A New System of slavery, The Export of Indian Labour Overseas, 1830-1920, London, Hansib Publishing Limited

Walsh, Ben, Case Study 3 Background: The End of the British Empire in India. (Retrieved from Archive resource) https://www.nationalarchives.gov.uk/education/empire/g3/cs3/background.htm

Williams, B.A.E. Wynn, 1951, The Kingsway Histories, Book Two, London

https://www.nationalarchives.gov.uk/help-with-your-research/research-guides/indian-indentured-labourers/

https://www.bbc.co.uk/bitesize/guides/zy7fr82/revision/1

http://www.georgetownsvgrevisited.co.uk/indentees-who-were-they.php

https://economictimes.indiatimes.com/mysterious-chapattis-and-nightrunners-of-the-rising/articleshow/1907480.cms?from=mdr Vikram, 2007

https://www.striking-women.org/module/map-major-south-asian-migration-flows/indentured-labour-south-asia-1834-1917#:~:text=The%20indentured%20workers%20sought%20to,British%20colonial%20rule%20in%20India

https://en.wikipedia.org/wiki/Famine_in_India#:~:text=Millions%20died%20from%201850%20to,%2Dcentury%20between%201871%E2%80%931921.

Indian indenture system – Wikipedia (2021)

https://en.wikipedia.org/wiki/Indo-Vincentian (2021)

http://www.caribbean-atlas.com/en/themes/waves-of-colonization-and-control-in-the-caribbean/waves-of-colonization/the-experience-of-indian-indenture-in-trinidad-arrival-and-settlement.html

Waweru, Nduta, 2018, Here's proof that Africans settled in South America long before Columbus' voyage https://face2faceafrica.com/article/heres-proof-that-africans-settled-in-south-america-long-be

Woolfe, Tao, 1992, Sun-Sentinel https://www.sun-sentinel.com/news/fl-xpm-1992-02-21-9201090772-story.html

https://www.indexmundi.com/saint_vincent_and_the_grenadines/demographics_profile

Source: CIA World Factbook

https://www.statista.com/statistics/1078947/saint-vincent-grenadines-agriculture-share-gdp/#:~:text=The%20agricultural%20sector%20in%20Saint,product%20(GDP)%20in%202018.

https://www.sciencedirect.com/science/article/pii/S0377027317306613, 1902 eruption Journal of Volcanology and Geothermal Research, Volume 356, 1 May 2018, Pages 183-199, The 1902–3 eruptions of the Soufriere, St Vincent: Impacts, relief and response, Blue Book correspondence for 1902 (BB1) and 1903

http://www.unesco.org/new/en/communication-and-information/memory-of-the-world/register/full-list-of-registered-heritage/registered-heritage-page-7/records-of-the-indian-indentured-labourers/

Places visited:

- India: Delhi, Varanasi, Hyderabad, Coimbatore, Karela, Cochi, Tamil Nadu etc

- St. Vincent and the Grenadines

- Trinidad and Tobago

- The United Kingdom

Samples of the Register of Indians' Pages

Spreadsheet Samples Of Register of Indians

See next page

Colonial Number	Name	Age	Sex	Height	Father	Ship Number	Zilla or District	Village	Estate Allotted	Notes
1087	Hurbosia	26	F		Ajmaree	18	Patna	Mosowree Mohajpore	Lot 14 Estate	Took 10 pounds 29/9/1879
1088	Sewgiah	5	F		Chamon	20	Patna	Mosowree Mohajpore	Lot 14 Estate	Took 10 pounds 30 Aug 1879
1089	Mynoah	3	F		Chamon	21	Patna	Mosowree Mohajpore	Lot 14 Estate	
1090	Khodabux	20	M		Nozibkhan	393	Azimghur	Nujumahad Patela	Lot 14 Estate	Took 10 pounds 6 Sept 1879
1091	Dookha (Khodabux)	24	M		Goferkhan	276	Chapra	Tajpore	Lot 14 Estate	Took 10 pounds 10 May 1880
1092	Fookeeraj (Dookha)	24	M		Narein	61	Modaferpoor	Busara Nahon	Lot 14 Estate	Took 10 pounds 12 Aug 1879
1093	Pookeera	35	M		Nunhoo	100	Modaferpoor	Tihot Noabazar	Lot 14 Estate	Took 10 pounds 11 Jun 1881
1094	Ropun	27	M		Dumur	224	Hazarebag	Mannickdeha? Naowaree	Lot 14 Estate	Took 10 pounds 22 Nov 1879
1095	Nanoah	30	M		Kurtoo	226	Hazarebag	Hannickdeha? Rama	Lot 14 Estate	
1096	Durson	26	M		Dhowtal	228	Modaferpoor	Pauloah? Hatee	Lot 14 Estate	Took 10 pounds 23 Aug 1879

Colonial Number	Name	Age	Sex	Height	Father	Ship Number	Zilla or District	Village	Estate Allotted	Notes
1097	Ressesur	30	M		Persad	362	Jounpore	Meashpore Nopara	Lot 14 Estate	
1098	Dabee	18	M		Badul	52	Ranchi	Ranchi Foreedpore	Lot 14 Estate	Took 10 pound 23 Aug 1879
1099	Toolsee	28	M		Ramchurn	66	Chapra	Peersa Amnour	Lot 14 Estate	
1100	Volgaloo	29	M		Lalasaw	51	Patna	Saborkatoa	Lot 14 Estate	Took 10 pound 30 Aug 1879
1101	Chamon	29	M		Ghurboo	17	Patna	Mosowree Mohajpore	Lot 14 Estate	Took 10 pound 29 Sept 1879
1102	Bhuggoo	28	M		Bhurosee	120	Modafer-pore	Basara Narhon	Lot 14 Estate	Took 10 pounds 29 ?9 1879
1103	Beharee	25	M		Gomcheer	144	Hazarebag	Khuruck deha Daronda	Lot 14 Estate	Took 10 pound 8 Sept 1879
1104	Seelokee	25	M		Dosoorgu	225	Hazarebag	Khuruck deha Vorkota	Lot 14 Estate	
1105	Bondhoy	23	M		Gopalroy	223	Hazarebag	Hazarebag Barwaree	Lot 14 Estate	

Colonial Number	Name	Age	Sex	Height	Father	Ship Number	Zilla or District	Village	Estate Allotted	Notes
1106	Sreelochum	9	M		Chamon	19	Patna	Mosowree Mohajpore	Lot 14 Estate	Took 10 pounds 20/9/1879
1107	Lutchmon	30	M		Greedharee	203	Gazepore	Bulleah Hurcha	Tourama Estate	Took 10 pounds 10 May 1880
1108	Runglaul	22	M		Sewdoss	121	Bhagulpore	Modapore Paroarer	Tourama Estate	Took 10 pounds 10 May 1881
1109	Kasie	30	M		Nakha	204	Gya	Arowh Ghogaila	Tourama Estate	Took 10 pounds 10 May 1882
1110	Jhugroo	26	M		Sunkur	13	Gazepoor	Johorabad Bahadur-gunge	Tourama Estate	Took 10 pounds 10 May 1883
1111	Bahadoor	23	M		Ramloll	146	Monghyr	Monghyr Balia	Tourama Estate	Took 10 pounds 10 May 1884
1112	Sewdoss	30	M		Jowdhon	196	Jounpore	Baragon Satowria	Tourama Estate	Took 10 pounds 10 May 1885
1113	Kullar	24	M		Sokhun	480	Monghyr	Mapore Ne-hadowlee	Tourama Estate	
1114	Chamon	26	M		Dosoruth	448	Gya	Jehana Sorabee	Tourama Estate	
1115	Sew	30	M		Bundoo	423	Benares	Chatgunge Lolapore	Tourama Estate	

Colonial Number	Name	Age	Sex	Height	Father	Ship Number	Zilla or District	Village	Estate Allotted	Notes
1116	Greedharee	21	M		Pram	222	Monghyr	Monghyr Indros	Tourama Estate	Took 10 pound 23 Aug 1879
1117	Jeetun	29	M		Moniaree	33	Monghyr	Amrathoo Chuck-under	Tourama Estate	Took 10 pounds 10 May 1880
1118	Kosohur	29	M		Hurloll	264	Arrah	Behela Dhonia	Tourama Estate	
1119	Ramdehal	27	M		Nakoo	277	Benares	Ardalebazar Sodekapara	Tourama Estate	
1120	Babooah	22	M		Peerbun	272	Allahabad	Motee-gunge	Tourama Estate	
1121	Neerunjunsing	26	M		Sewsahie	14	Arrah	Bhojpore Dormon	Tourama Estate	Took 10 pounds 10 May 1880
1122	Anondia	26	M		Emrith	164	Gazeepore	Jomonia Barrah	Tourama Estate	
1123	Somaria	26	F		Ablack	245	Patna	Foolway	Tourama Estate	
1124	Somaria	30	F		Boodhoo	376	Jounpore	Jounpore Marie	Tourama Estate	
1125	Luckeah	24	M		Doorbul	250	Chapra	Bajra Sa-habgung	Tourama Estate	Took 10 pounds 10 May 1880

Colonial Number	Name	Age	Sex	Height	Father	Ship Number	Zilla or District	Village	Estate Allotted	Notes
1126	Boodhanee	25	M		Selote	377	Jounpore	Jounpore Tearce	Tourama Estate	
1127	Sadoo	25	M		Kosie	320	Sewree	Riepore	Tourama Estate	Took 10 pounds 10 May 1880
2583	Ramphul	30	M	5' 5"	Bhowani Roy	51			Argyle	Scar R shin
2584	Anopia	25	F	5' 1.5"	Thakoor	52			Argyle	Tattoo both forearm
2585	Kalloo	9	M		Ramphul	53			Argyle	
2586	Bhugmonti	3	F		Ramphul	54			Argyle	
2587	Sewdin	30	M	5' 1"	Jookhoo	55			Argyle	Scar L shin
2588	Neerohoo	24	M	5' 6"	Dhouraj	56			Argyle	Scar L knee
2589	Mulki	22	F	4' 11"	Ramdin	57			Argyle	Scar L forearm
2590	Soobhagea	27	F	4' 6"	Zorap	58			Argyle	Tattoo both arms
2591	Mohango	24	M	5' 7.5"	Jewlaul	59			Argyle	Scar R side belly
2592	Pursoo	17	M	5' 2"	Issree	60			Argyle	R small finger defective
2593	Juggou	30	M	5' 2.5"	Porowtee?	61			Mt. Wynn	Moles on chest
2594	Mogayah	20	M	5' 1"	Kissona	62			Mt. Wynn	Scar left foot

Colonial Number	Name	Age	Sex	Height	Father	Ship Number	Zilla or District	Village	Estate Allotted	Notes
2595	Lugnee	20	F	4' 8.5"	Gheerawo	63			Colonarie	Tattoo both arms
2596	Puttoolaul	24	M	5' 4"	Laulmon	64			Argyle	Scar L shin
2597	Goordin	22	M	5' 5.5"	Oree	65			Calder	Pock marked
2598	Rampersad	20	M	5' 3"	Boyjhauth	66			Argyle	Scar R temple
2599	Seetul	20	M	5' 5"	Sewdin	67			Argyle	Scar R knee
2600	Thakoor	26	M	5' 4"	Sewchurn	68			Argyle	Scar L knee
2601	Kallidin	20	M	5' 5"	Mataie	69			Argyle	Scar L knee
2602	Joymonea	24	F	4' 11"	Sewbhojun	70			Argyle	Pock marked
2603	Goneshee	20	M	5' 4"	Dabee	71			Argyle	Scar loin
2604	Bhuggon	28	M	4' 10"	Burhoo	72			Bellair	Pock marked
2605	Goptar	20	M	5' 4"	Gunga	73			Carapan	Scar below left eye
2606	Chandalli	18	M	5' 1"	Bachaie	74			Bellair	Pock marked
2607	Sirtajkoor	20	F	4' 11"	Damarkee	75			Argyle	Tattoo both arms
2608	Joharon	22	F	4' 10"	Muckdom-box	76			Argyle	Tattoo both arms
2609	Ramdaya	24	F	5' 4"	Bhoyjoo	77			Cane Grove	Tattoo both arms

Colonial Number	Name	Age	Sex	Height	Father	Ship Number	Zilla or District	Village	Estate Allotted	Notes
2610	Bootawo	25	F	4' 10"	Rughoolun	78			Argyle	Tattoo both arms
2611	Seetaz	28	F	5' 0"	Ramsahaie	79			Bellair	Pock marked
2612	Sewbaluck	35	M	5' 3"	Wooduth	80			Cane Grove	Wart L cheek
2613	Ameer	22	M	5' 3"	Baj	81			Cane Grove	Scar L rib
2614	Sooburnee	40	F	4' 8.5"	Ahlum	82			Cane Grove	none
2615	Azim	28	M	5' 1"	Chands	83			Cane Grove	Scar left thigh
2616	Monglee	25	F	4' 10.5"	Dhonee	84			Cane Grove	Scar left knee
2617	Jhoomuck	28	M	5' 2"	Shoomon	85			Bellair	Pock marked
2618	Dillshair	25	M	5' 2.5"	Buck-tamon?	86			Argyle	Scar left indexer
2619	Dewkising	26	M	5' 4"	Shibhurn Sing	87			Argyle	Scar R cheek
2620	Maria	30	F	4' 7"	Sofferalli	88			Bellair	Moles on forehead
2621	Goribuni	5	F		Nookhan	89			Bellair	
2622	Golab	25	M	5' 1"	Saybock	90			Cane Grove	Scar L shin
2623	Dassea	22	F	5' 0"	Bohoree	91			Cane Grove	Scar L arm

Appendix III
Sample of Gazette pages

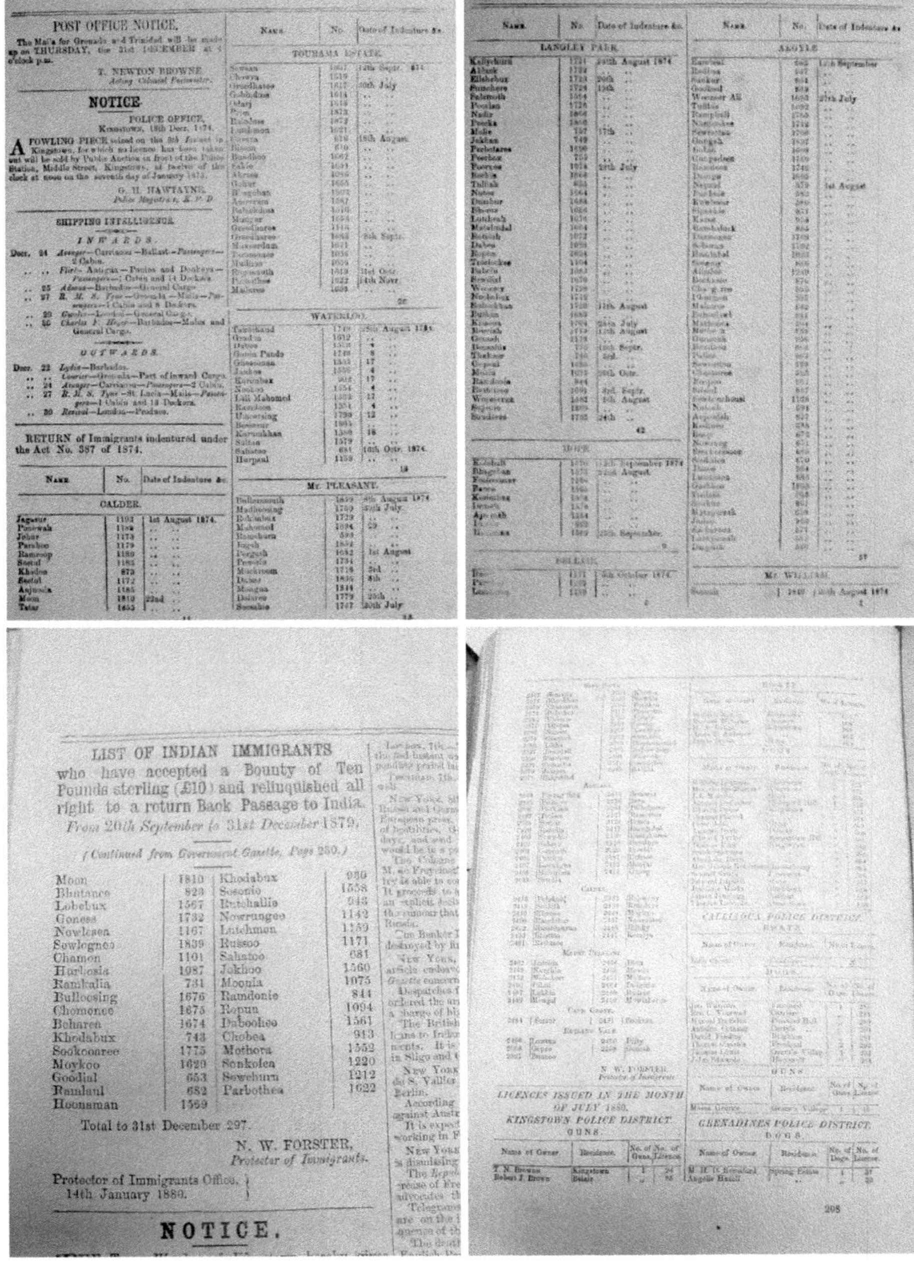

SVG Indian Heritage Foundation Registration

Form 9

COMPANIES ACT OF 1994
(Sections 69 & 77)

NOTICE OF DIRECTORS
OR
NOTICE OF CHANGE OF DIRECTORS

1. Name of Company

SVG INDIAN HERITAGE FOUNDATION INC.

2. Company No.

5 7 2007

3. Notice is given that on the 19ᵗʰ day of February, 2007 the following person(s) was/were appointed director(s)

Name	Address	Occupation
Elmore C. Gaymes	Layou, St. Vincent	Teacher
Branson D. Thomas	Argyle, St. Vincent	Civil Servant
Jannis A. Deane	Cane Hall, St. Vincent	Lecturer
Cheryl G. Rodriguez	Yambou, St. Vincent	Bank Official
Junior Bacchus *(no middle initial)*	Dauphine, St. Vincent	Proprietor
Lenroy D. Thomas	Richland Park, St. Vincent	Special Project Director
Denzil C. Bacchus	Villa, St. Vincent	Jeweller

4. Notice is given that on the   day of   ,   the following person(s) ceased to hold office as director(s)

Name	Address	Occupation
N/A	N/A	N/A

5. The directors of the company as of this date are:

Name	Address	Occupation
Elmore C. Gaymes	Layou, St. Vincent	Teacher
Branson D. Thomas	Argyle, St. Vincent	Civil Servant
Jannis A. Deane	Cane Hall, St. Vincent	Lecturer
Cheryl G. Rodriguez	Yambou, St. Vincent	Bank Official
Junior Bacchus *(no middle initial)*	Dauphine, St. Vincent	Proprietor
Lenroy D. Thomas	Richland Park, St. Vincent	Special Project Director
Denzil C. Bacchus	Villa, St. Vincent	Jeweller

Date	Signature	Title
12ᵀᴴ April, 2007	JANNIS AGNES DEANE	INCORPORATOR

C
RECEIVED
Below this line for Registry use only
I
P   27 APR 2007
517064